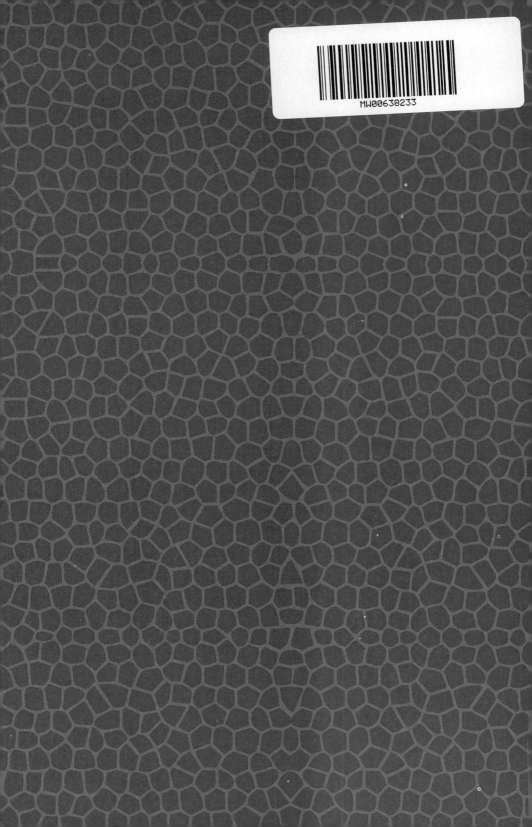

MW00638233

RESILIENCE

MOSAICA PRESS

RESILIENCE

A Jewish Guide to Facing Adversity,
Fostering Strength, and Living Your Best Life

LESLIE M. GUTMAN, PHD

Published by Mosaica Press, Inc.
www.mosaicapress.com
info@mosaicapress.com

In loving memory of

Connie *bas* Rose

A model of resilience, creativity, generosity,
integrity, and compassion.
May her good deeds be an inspiration.

Dedicated by
DANIEL MORRISON AND RIKI WEINSTEIN
AND FAMILY

Dedicated in honor of the author,
our beloved sister and sister-in-law

Leslie and her family

With love, respect, and deep affection

CHAIM AND BETH BROODO

Thank you to our friend, Leslie,
for writing this wonderful and vital book on resilience.
May our three beautiful daughters,

Olivia, Hannah, and Adina

continue to grow into Torah as loving,
balanced, and resilient women.

PERRY AND ANGELA DOWELL

Dedicated in honor of the memory
of all our loved ones, in honor of all our loved ones,
and to our dear friend and author of this book.

JONNY AND ALISON SOLOMON

TABLE OF CONTENTS

PREFACE

According to Jewish belief, everyone has his own *pekeleh* (baggage). In fact, we are born with two sets:

- One set is full of the challenges that we face in our lifetime.
- The other set is filled with the advantages, talents, and abilities that we are given to endure those challenges.

Each person's *pekeleh* is designed uniquely for them; no test is more than we can handle, yet each one still has the potential to bring out an improved version of ourselves. While the first set of baggage is opened for us, the second set we need to open on our own. Resilience is comparable to opening the second set of baggage in order to adapt to the challenges presented in the first. According to Rabbi Moshe Chaim Luzzatto, the purpose of life is "to perform mitzvos, to serve, and to withstand tests."[1] Resilience, which involves utilizing our strengths in order to effectively cope with and learn from life's challenges, may thus be considered one of our most important lifelong tasks.

Adversity is a tie that binds us; almost everyone has suffered at some point or another. My own *pekeleh* includes, among other things, having undergone a divorce at the same time that my sister was diagnosed with cancer. Whatever your *pekeleh*, resilience is within your grasp. We can all do it. This book is intended to offer a better understanding of how

---

1   M. C. Luzzatto, *Path of the Just*, trans. Silverstein (New York: Feldheim Publishers, 2004).

to confront life's setbacks and foster the different strengths that exist within all of us.

According to the Talmud, when we are in the womb, God assigns a personal angel to each and every one of us, who then teaches us the Torah in its entirety.[2] Just before our birth, this angel gives us a little tap on the mouth, and everything we learned in the womb is "forgotten." (Some suggest that this is the reason we have a philtrum, the small indentation in the skin beneath the nose!)

The point is that the knowledge of the Torah remains dormant within each of us, awakening as we learn and live in this world. As Rabbi Joseph B. Soloveitchik wrote, "When a Jew studies Torah, he is confronted with something...familiar, because he has already studied it and the knowledge was stored up in the recesses of his memory; the Torah became a part of him."[3]

This is incredibly empowering. What this means is that we naturally possess all the knowledge and ability we need within ourselves to live our life to its greatest potential. Throughout our life's journey, we can recollect what we instinctively understand and rediscover what we are meant to achieve. In other words, we can all live our best lives.

RESILIENCE IN A TIME OF UNCERTAINTY AND CHANGE

As this book goes to print, we are in the midst of the coronavirus crisis. The timely nature of this book's publication was not planned, although it is not coincidental by any means. As others have duly noted, this is the first time in recent history when we have been united, as a global population, facing the same adversary.

While we stand together, we must remember that this crisis also sets individuals and families apart, in terms of their experiences of suffering. For many, this is a stressful time when we have restricted access to food and other necessities, worries about schooling and finances, and physical isolation from family and friends. For a significant number,

---

2   N. Weinberg, *What the Angel Taught You* (Jerusalem: Shaar Press, 2003).

3   J. B. Soloveitchik, "Redemption, Prayer, Talmud Torah," *Tradition: A Journal of Orthodox Jewish Thought*, vol. 17, no. 2 (1978): 55–72.

COVID-19 has brought tragedy in the form of the unexpected and often lonely death of a loved one. Others have encountered financial hardship. For some, social isolation and the uncontrollable nature of this crisis have exacerbated existing trauma and adversity. Mental health problems may become more acute, steering some to a challenging place. Struggling relationships may be pushed over the edge, leading to later resentment, estrangement, or divorce. What is important to focus on now is how we can reduce our exposure to additional stresses and imbue resilience in ourselves and our loved ones so we can deal with the uncertainty that faces us now and in the future.

While COVID-19 seems to have caught most of us by surprise, for the past decade or so, researchers have been studying societal resilience in response to widespread catastrophes, such as natural disasters, pandemic flu, and terrorism. In one review of studies representing approximately thirteen million disaster-exposed civilians of adult age, strong social support was shown to be the key ingredient for a resilient outcome.[4] There is an abundance of research highlighting the importance of social support for our physical and psychological health, especially in times of trauma. Social support increases our resilience by improving our ability to cope effectively with challenges as well as reducing the harmful effects of our brain's neurochemical responses to stress.[5]

Social support can be practical, expressed in acts of kindness and/or financial assistance, or emotional, in the giving and receiving of love. In both instances, social support means that we have people whom we can rely on during difficult times as well as celebrate with during joyous occasions. Social support conveys that we are not alone and have social ties to a larger community. Social support reminds us that someone cares about and loves us. Social support signifies that we are important to someone and belong to something greater than ourselves.

---

4   Rodriguez-Llanes, Jose Manuel, Femke Vos, and Debarati Guha-Sapir, "Measuring psychological resilience to disasters: are evidence-based indicators an achievable goal?" *Environmental Health* 12.1 (2013): 115.

5   F. Ozbay, D. C. Johnson, E. Dimoulas, C. A. Morgan III, D. Charney, and S. Southwick, "Social support and resilience to stress: from neurobiology to clinical practice," *Psychiatry* (Edgmont), 4(5) (2007): 35–40.

This is the takeaway message of this challenging time: connection matters. During the pandemic, we have witnessed this daily, with friends and strangers sharing their food and other supplies, communities learning and davening together through video conferencing, neighbors singing *Shalom Aleichem* from their porches, and people celebrating *simchahs* from their balconies. The real-life examples are boundless, but the common denominator is the same: our mitzvos are the vehicle through which we connect with one another and, in turn, with God. In fact, the Hebrew word *mitzvah*, "commandment," is associated with the Aramaic word *tzavta*, which means "connection" or "togetherness."[6] We, who are commanded (*metzuveh*), become one with God, our Commander (*Metzaveh*).[7] Through our mitzvos, we become part of something infinitely greater than ourselves; we become a partner with God.

In this global phenomenon, each of us has a crucial role to play. One of the central tenets of Judaism is that every mitzvah we do ascends above to Heaven and has far-reaching consequences for the universe.[8] The concept of *olam katan* signifies that each person is a microcosm of the entire world and our actions influence the events of the macrocosmic universe around us. In our own way, we can change the world for the better through the refinement of our own thoughts and actions.

There is a story told in the name of the Chafetz Chaim, who once said that he dreamed of perfecting the entire world. When he saw that this was overly ambitious, he focused instead on changing his country of Poland. When this was beyond his reach, he decided on changing his small village. When this seemed impossible, he settled on changing the synagogue where he prayed and learned. He soon realized that the only person he could change was himself. In his lifetime, he wrote many works that have become the cornerstone of Torah observance.

---

6   *Shelah Hakadosh, Yoma, Derech Chaim Tochachas Mussar* (16).

7   Y. Hartman and O. C. Levene, *Jewish Wisdom in the Numbers* (New York: Mesorah Publications, 2013).

8   S. M. Riachi, *The Elucidated Tomer Devorah: Learning Compassion through Hashem's 13 Attributes of Mercy* (New York: Feldheim, 2015).

By changing himself, the Chafetz Chaim indeed succeeded in changing the entire world.

The significance of our actions in preventing infection to others and ourselves has been emphasized by the government and medical profession, including the careful washing of our hands, social distancing, and the wearing of face masks. Similarly, our prayers are also necessary for healing and redemption. While physically isolated, many of us connect to God on our own, in the absence of communal prayer. In the seclusion of our own home, the dual conflictual nature of humankind described in Rabbi Soloveitchik's *Lonely Man of Faith*[9] seems to have somewhat reconciled. Our drive to dominate our environment through material gains has been suppressed, and we are left with a spiritual quest for meaning and understanding. The absence of distraction from material acquisition provides us with the unique opportunity to reflect on who we really are and who we want to strive to become.

This introspection is crucial for our growth and progression as individuals and as a nation. Rabbi Chaim of Volozhin writes that the true Temple is in the heart of man.[10] Our Holy Temple in Jerusalem was only an instrument that served our inner Temple, which is the sanctity of our heart.[11] With this in mind, the building of our outer Temple depends on the building our own inner Temple, which involves offering the service of our heart wholeheartedly to God.[12] During this time, when our outer worlds have narrowed through restricted social gatherings and physical travel, we are given the chance to expand our inner relationship with God, expressed through the sincerity of our prayer and mitzvos, our acts of loving-kindness, and our generosity to others.

We are now immersed in a time of uncertainty and change. It may be difficult, as such times often bring a sense of loss, insecurity, and complication. With uncertainty, however, can come unexpected opportunity. Change can bring hope for a new beginning, a renewed connection

---

9   J. B. Soloveitchik, *The Lonely Man of Faith* (New York: Image, 2009).
10   E. E. Dessler, *Strive for Truth! Part 3*, trans. A. Carmell (Jerusalem: Feldheim, 1978).
11   Ibid.
12   Ibid.

with one another and God, and a greater realization of what is possible and what we can achieve. Our resilience is essential to successfully navigating through this challenging period as well as any other that life presents us. It is my hope that *Resilience* provides you with a greater understanding of how to face setbacks with courage and fortitude, foster your individual and collective strengths, and strive to reach your utmost aspirations and potentialities, living life to the fullest.

Leslie Morrison Gutman
London, England
October 2020

ACKNOWLEDGMENTS

This book began as a thought that was developed and nurtured until it was ready to be expressed and shared, in the right way and at the right point in time.

I am extremely grateful to those who have been instrumental in the creation and publication of this book. Many thanks to Rabbi Yaacov Haber and Rabbi Doron Kornbluth for their editorial direction, and to the staff at Mosaica Press—including Sherie Gross for her oversight of the project, Meira Lawrence for her expert copyediting, Adina Edelman for her careful proofreading, Rayzel Broyde for her creative art design, and Brocha Mirel Strizower for her meticulous typesetting—transforming this book into a reality.

My humble gratitude is expressed to Rabbi Dr. Akiva Tatz, Rebbetzin Shira Smiles, and Dr. Tal Ben-Shahar for their words of endorsement, with particular thanks to Rabbi Dr. Akiva Tatz for his invaluable advice and guidance in the early stages of my writing. I am further indebted to those extraordinary, courageous individuals (you know who you are!) who openly shared their personal stories of resilience with me. Their own experiences illuminate this book, highlighting their fortitude and strengthening others. My heartfelt appreciation must also be conveyed to family and friends who contributed suggestions on the content and writing, provided verbal encouragement, and offered dedications.

I am very blessed to have many people in my life who have positively impacted my understanding and experience of resilience, including my family and *rabbanim*, mentors, teachers, colleagues, and friends, past and present.

One couple deserves particular mention—Rabbi Avraham and Rebbetzin Bayla Jacobovitz. They are truly one of a kind, and are responsible for having helped me find my path so many times that I've lost count. Both have contributed to this book, not only in reading and remarking on earlier versions, but, most importantly, imbuing me with the spiritual resilience to write it in the first place!

How can one ever truly express the depth of their gratitude to their family for what has been given, unconditionally and in love? My parents, Dr. Dan Morrison and Dr. Riki Weinstein and Mr. Frank and Mrs. Elaine Rosenbaum, are my stronghold and have never wavered in their love, acceptance, and support of me. My in-laws, Rabbi Avraham and Mrs. Helen Abrahami, have provided me with a family far from my native home. My brother-in-law and sister (and best friend), Chaim and Beth Broodo, have always been there for me and freely allowed me to share their own stories of resilience in this book.

My beloved husband, Adam Abrahami, is my everything and partner in all that we create. We pray to the Almighty that we live long, healthy, meaningful, and happy lives together to the fullest, reaching our spiritual potential and accomplishing our unique mission. We beseech our Creator that our cherished children—Talia Shoshana, Michael Chaim, Eliyahu, Natanel Shlomo, and Shmuel Avraham, and our dear son-in-law Eliyahu Yosef Meir—live long lives as Torah-observant, happy, healthy, and productive individuals who continue to bring us much *nachas* and *simchahs*. "May we have learned children and grandchildren, who dazzle the world with Torah and goodness and ensure that the glow of our lives never grow dim."

Hakadosh Baruch Hu, You have given me what I needed to write and publish this book, and I am eternally grateful to You for all Your blessings. I pray to You that these words and their meaning will reach a far and wide audience—and bring only goodness, empowering and strengthening all who read them.

INTRODUCTION

"If statistics are right, the Jews constitute but
one percent of the human race. It suggests a
nebulous dim puff of stardust lost in the blaze
of the Milky Way. Properly, the Jew ought
hardly to be heard of, but he is heard of, has
always been heard of. He is as prominent
on the planet as any other people, and his
commercial importance is extravagantly out
of proportion to the smallness of his bulk. His
contributions to the world's list of great names
in literature, science, art, music, finance,
medicine, and abstruse learning are also way
out of proportion to the weakness of his
numbers. He has made a marvelous fight in
this world, in all the ages; and has done it with
his hands tied behind him."[1]

Mark Twain

"The Jews, however, are beyond all doubt the
strongest, toughest, and purest race at present

---

1   Mark Twain, "Concerning the Jews," *Harper's Magazine*, 1899.

> living in Europe; they know how to succeed even
> under the worst conditions (in fact better than
> under favorable ones)."[2]
>
> Friedrich Nietzche

Resilience is exemplified in our Jewish heritage and history.

Our Patriarchs and Matriarchs overcame the most challenging hardships. Throughout history, the Jewish People have encountered numerous periods when our very existence was at stake, yet we have survived and even prospered. Many of our holidays celebrate the resilience of the Jewish People in maintaining our traditions throughout thousands of years of exile despite the efforts of dominant civilizations to enslave, assimilate, convert, or destroy us. In this sense, collective resilience exists among the Jewish People, Klal Yisrael, through our shared history and faith.[3]

While we possess spiritual and historical resilience as a nation, as individuals, we often struggle to cope with the problems of modern society. One paradox of our world today is that we have more technological advances and luxuries than any period in history, yet financial, social, and personal problems are still present. Despite having a world of knowledge at our fingertips, we are often unsure how to respond to the inevitable problems and pitfalls of life.

While God controls the specific difficulties that we may face in this world, we control our responses to those challenges. How we handle tough times is often a reflection of how we experience life. Do we live in denial? Do we surrender to hardship and despair? Do we struggle, barely keeping our heads above the water? Do we confront difficult circumstances? Do we rebuild our lives?

Psychological research has outlined at least four potential responses to serious misfortune:[4]

---

2   Friedrich Nietzche, German philosopher, 1844–1900.

3   Rabbi Berel Wein, "The Strong and the Weak," http://www.torah.org/learning/rabbi-wein/5767/chanukah.html.

4   V. E. O'Leary and J. R. Ickovics, "Resilience and thriving in response to challenge: an

1. **Suffering:** Our mental and physical health seriously suffers.
2. **Survival:** We survive but experience a decline in some aspects of life.
3. **Resilience:** We heal from trauma and move forward in a positive way.[5]
4. **Post-traumatic growth:** We experience positive growth as a consequence of overcoming trauma, leading to an improvement in our life.[6]

These last two possible responses are not mutually exclusive and often overlap.[7] While resilience focuses on the process of healing and recovery during trauma, post-traumatic growth (also known as flourishing or thriving) focuses on positive transformation in the aftermath of trauma.

While some of us are naturally more likely to experience resilience than others because of the way we view the world, the capacity for resilience exists within all of us. We are not *born* resilient, we are *made* resilient. By understanding the characteristics and mechanisms of resilience, we can learn how to promote resilience in ourselves and our loved ones.

> We are not *born* resilient, we are *made* resilient.

HOW TO USE THIS BOOK

Resilience is an active practice that we engage in every day through the choices we make for ourselves and through our relationships with others. This book is written as a guide to help readers chart a more resilient path. Alongside academic research, this book contains illuminations from the Torah and its scholars, as well as Jewish spirituality,

---

opportunity for a paradigm shift in women's health," *Women's Health* (Hillsdale, NJ), 1(2) (1995): 121–142.

5   G. A. Bonanno, "Loss, trauma, and human resilience: Have we underestimated the human capacity to thrive after extremely aversive events?" *American Psychologist*, 59(1) (2004): 20.

6   C. S. Carver, "Resilience and thriving: Issues, models, and linkages," *Journal of Social Issues*, 54(2) (1998): 245–266.

7   B. W. Smith, J. Dalen, K. Wiggins, E. Tooley, P. Christopher, and J. Bernard, "The brief resilience scale: assessing the ability to bounce back," *International Journal of Behavioral Medicine*, 15(3) (2008): 194–200.

thought, and history. There are also personal stories of resilience from different individuals, as well as practical exercises teaching resilience-building strategies.

This book is organized into five main parts:

- What is resilience?
- What is adversity?
- What are the major tests facing us today?
- What fosters resilience?
- What is post-traumatic growth?

Three important caveats need to be considered when reading this book.

- This book provides an overview of research on resilience, although many more studies exist and there continues to be new research. Similar to developing resilience, learning about it is a lifelong process.
- The Jewish perspective discussed in this book merely skims the surface of the depth, complexity, and beauty that is contained within classic Judaism.
- Most importantly, this book is intended to be a guide. It is not a substitute for guidance from a rabbi or for professional advice, diagnosis, and treatment from a medical doctor, psychologist, or other qualified health-care provider.

Chapter One

WHAT IS RESILIENCE?

Imagine a rubber ball, perfectly round and smooth. This ball is thrown against a surface and it bounces right back, without an indication of its previous blow. This is often a conceptualization of resilience: toughness, springing back into shape, and recovering quickly from trauma. Yet, a rubber ball is not an appropriate metaphor for resilience. When we undergo adversity, we are not the same as before. We fundamentally change with the experience; we can learn, grow, and rebuild. Resilience is an essential set of skills that we can improve over time, enabling us to transform setbacks into new opportunities and pathways. Resilience is not about bouncing *back* but rather bouncing *forward* into a better version of ourselves.

> Resilience is not about bouncing *back* but rather bouncing *forward* into a better version of ourselves.

Resilience necessitates two coexisting conditions.[1]

---

1   A. S. Masten and J. D. Coatsworth, "The development of competence in favorable and unfavorable environments: Lessons from research on successful children." *American Psychologist*, 53(2) (1998): 205.

- Facing a serious adversity or experiencing a traumatic event. Resilience is not about surmounting minor stumbling blocks.
- Successfully adapting to a new circumstance. What is considered a marker of "successful adaptation" depends on the specific challenge. For someone coping with divorce, it might mean taking on new opportunities, establishing different routines and responsibilities, and developing a supportive network of family and friends. For someone experiencing a catastrophe, such as war, it might mean mere survival.

An example of resilience is my sister. When she was nursing her third child, she found some lumps in her breast. She dismissed these suspicious lumps as related to her breastfeeding. When, a few months later, she went for a breast scan at the urging of our father, a diagnosis of stage 3C breast cancer was revealed. She was rushed into an emergency double mastectomy and endured months of chemotherapy, radiation, and a powerful medicine called Herceptin. More than ten years later, she is now a breast cancer survivor. She also facilitates Cancer Support Services at Jewish Families Services in Dallas, Texas. Since her tenure in this position, she has helped many women. It is not an easy job for her, as it serves as a daily reminder of her vulnerability. While she sometimes feels a sense of anxiety regarding the unforeseeable future, she also feels tremendous gratitude to God for her life and the gift of loving and raising her three children with her husband. She is a beacon of light, shining her spiritual strength and courage as a message of hope to those around her.

Let us now consider the two coexisting conditions of resilience.

FACING AN ADVERSITY OR EXPERIENCING A TRAUMATIC EVENT

Avraham Avinu was given not one but ten successive trials from God. He withstood them all, becoming closer to God in the process. Avram (later to be known as Avraham) first responded to God's call to leave his homeland and father's house to go to the land of Canaan. In the land of Canaan, Avram faced even more challenges. When he was given the commandment of circumcision, Avram was given a new, more global life mission and renamed Avraham, which means "the father of multitudes." Avraham was then confronted with what many consider his most difficult test of all. God told Avraham: "Take your son, your favored one, Yitzchak, whom you love, and go to the land of Moriah, and offer him there as a burnt offering on one of the heights that I point to you."[2] Avraham and his beloved son Yitzchak traveled to the "land of Moriah." As Avraham raised the knife, an angel stopped him at the last moment. "Do not raise your hand to the boy, or do anything to him," the angel proclaimed. "For now I know that you fear God, since you have not withheld your son, your favored one, from Me."[3]

The ten tests of Avraham raise some pivotal questions about resilience:

- Why is facing a serious life challenge necessary for resilience?
- Can we build resilience through our handling of day-to-day hassles?

Resilience, by its very nature, necessitates successful adjustment to a new circumstance. When we experience a traumatic event, it is game-changing. It shakes us to the very core of our being. In order to be resilient, we must break old habits. We must move on from those people, places, and patterns of behavior that are preventing our growth. An interesting case in point occurs after the sin of the Golden Calf when God told Moshe that the Jewish nation is a "stiff-necked people" and He will destroy us. According to Rabbi Eliyahu Eliezer Dessler, being stiff-necked is similar to being obstinate and not listening to our hearts.[4] Moshe responded with self-sacrificing prayer, giving himself up for death. But all this gained only a temporary respite, according to *Ramban*.[5] The long-term remedy was Moshe's breaking of the tablets. "I took hold of the two tablets and I threw them down from my two hands and I broke them in front of your eyes."[6] Imagine viewing the earth-shattering sight of the holy tablets being broken by Moshe

2   *Bereishis* 22:2.
3   *Bereishis* 22:12.
4   E. E. Dessler, *Strive for Truth! Part 1*, trans. A. Carmell (Jerusalem: Feldheim, 1978).
5   *Shemos* 32:11.
6   *Devarim* 9:17.

himself, with "the divinely-written letters flying away."[7] This shocking experience forced the Jewish People to see the error of their ways and brought about a real change in their behavior.[8]

Similar to building a muscle, resilience takes time to develop. Learning how to successfully handle daily hassles allows us to flex our muscles (so to speak) and develops our capacity to overcome serious life challenges when they inevitably arise. Dealing with the everyday messiness of life, however, is unlikely to bring forth any significant life changes. With the exception of an embarrassing or funny memory, we tend to forget these incidents relatively quickly and proceed with our lives as before. So, while surmounting minor bumps in the road builds our capacity for resilience, swerving from these roadblocks is not enough to confer resilience, in and of itself.

In contrast, when we experience trauma, our survival and subsequent healing become the focal point of our lives. It is all hands on deck. We must harness every available resource, utilize our strengths, and uncover our hidden talents. We have the capacity to soar to heights of fortitude, resourcefulness, patience, and grace that we never even considered imaginable before. Our greatness emerges, not despite adversity but as a direct result of it. It is the difficulty inherent in the challenge itself that forces us to discover what would have otherwise remained concealed.

> Our greatness emerges, not despite adversity but as a direct result of it.

We can garner some insight into the significance of adversity through an examination of the different meanings of the Hebrew root of *nisayon* (test), which is *nes*.[9] There are two other meanings for *nes*: banner and miracle. In the Hebrew language, there are no coincidences. Every word reveals the essence of the item it describes. The question is: What is the connection among the meanings of test, banner, and miracle?

First, let us consider the meaning of a trial or test. Despite the appearance of randomness, nothing happens without a reason. Divine

---

7   E. E. Dessler, *Strive for Truth! Part 1*, trans. A. Carmell (Jerusalem: Feldheim, 1978), p. 192.

8   Ibid.

9   A. Tatz, *Living Inspired* (New York: Feldheim Publishers, 1993).

Providence, or *hashgachah pratis* in Hebrew, means that everything that takes place in the world is willed by God for a specific purpose. With this in mind, the basic Torah perspective is that whatever happens to us is purposeful and (ultimately) for our own good.

This doesn't mean that our lives will be easy. "Good" events are often seen as those that are comfortable and enjoyable, and "bad" events are seen as those that are difficult and unpleasant, but life cannot be viewed according to this simplistic dichotomy. Since God is pure, simple goodness, everything He creates is also good. There are two categories of good:[10]

- Revealed good is what we pray for and what we wish for our children.
- Concealed good is what involves suffering and what we wish to avoid.

It is often very difficult for us to understand how painful situations are considered "good." In our limited view, we are unable to comprehend the magnitude of events according to the entirety of existence. If we could, we would see that each event was perfectly designed for us to help us achieve our life's mission. As the Talmud teaches us: "A blessing is found only in something that is hidden from view."[11] In other words, when we open our eyes, we can see the blessing that is hidden in life's biggest challenges.

Next, let's consider the meaning of banner. A banner is a flag that is raised high and carries a special message. Our Sages inform us that when suffering comes to a person, he should examine his deeds.[12] When we are given a test, we are being taught a lesson from God. To understand its meaning, God will often send us a message in a way that directly relates to the area in which we need to improve. There is a principle in Judaism called *middah k'neged middah*, which is translated as "measure for measure," meaning that the punishment must be equal to the

---

10   *Tanya*, chap. 26, as cited in https://www.chabad.org/theJewishWoman/article_cdo/aid/402215/jewish/Two-Kinds-of-Good.htm.

11   *Tannis* 8b.

12   M. C. Luzzatto, *The Way of God*, trans. A. Kaplan (Jerusalem: Feldheim Publishers, 1996).

crime. In this sense, a test is a specific missive from God, encouraging us to explore our actions and consider whether we are following our chosen path.

Usually, tests happen for one of two reasons:

- Sometimes, a test is a punishment, given as an opportunity to correct our ways.
- Other times, such as in the case of Avraham, the purpose of a test is to awaken qualities within us that are dormant.

Despite our best efforts, however, we cannot always understand the specific meaning behind God's banner. Nevertheless, this should not diminish the intrinsic power of any test. Regardless of its meaning, "everything in life serves as a challenge and test to elevate us."[13] Therefore, the most important message concerns whether we utilize our challenges as opportunities for spiritual elevation.

What about the other meaning of *nes*, miracle? A miracle is the revelation of the Divine in our daily life. The purpose of a miracle is to remind us that God creates and rules the world. In the traditional Jewish perspective, the greatest miracle of history was the splitting of the Yam Suf (Sea of Reeds) during the Exodus from Egypt. Rabbi Sholom Noach Berezovsky, the Slonimer Rebbe,[14] comments on the verse, "The Israelites went into the sea on dry ground, the waters forming a wall for them on their right and on their left."[15] He relies on the interpretation of an earlier Chassidic Master, Rabbi Elimelech of Lizhensk, noting that after the splitting of the Yam Suf, the Jewish People still felt as though they were in the midst of the supernatural, even after they emerged onto dry land and returned to the realm of the ordinary. "The highest form of faith is the awareness that Israel achieved after our departure from slavery and the parting of the Yam Suf; that is the faith that every

---

13   M. C. Luzzatto, *Path of the Just*, trans. Silverstein (New York: Feldheim Publishers, 2004).
14   Author of *Nesivos Sholom*, a collection of Chassidic discourses on Jewish thought published in the latter half of the twentieth century.
15   *Shemos* 14:22.

aspect of our lives is miraculous, and that nothing is random and occurring simply of this world…"[16]

Miracles abound at every moment, for example, in the birth of a baby, the setting of the sun, and the wondrous nature that surrounds us. This is the paradox of our existence: we are so accustomed to the miracles we encounter in our daily lives that these are considered "ordinary" occurrences. We live oblivious to the miracles of life that remind us of God's constant presence. What is even more miraculous is that we are given a higher purpose—we can renew and repair this world through our growth and transformation. In this world, each person is designated with a certain role that only they can achieve. However, we often reach stumbling blocks, and we are unable to move forward. God gives us tests as a way of propelling us closer to reaching our true purpose. Life-changing, traumatic events challenge our assumptions and behaviors, compelling us to make the necessary adjustments that actualize our potential.

> God gives us tests as a way of propelling us closer to actualizing our potential.

This coincides with the essence of resilience. Research suggests that the human capacity to recover after traumatic events is far greater than we realize.[17] It is only through the experience of tragedy that we discover our aptitude for resilience. While we might consider resilience extraordinary, it arises from "ordinary magic," using only the normal capacities and resources that we rely on to function every day.[18]

Our capacity for resilience is cultivated through simple, fundamental human qualities and relationships. In this sense, "ordinary magic" is simply the miracles that surround us in our day-to-day existence. These miracles can be revealed through the optimism and hope we hold in our hearts, the gratitude we have for our lives, the love we give freely to our children, the kindness we demonstrate to others, and fundamentally,

---

16   Rabbi Elimelech of Lizhensk in *Noam Elimelech*, as cited in https://www.isralight.org/assets/ Text/RSS_yomyerushalayim06.html.

17   G. A. Bonanno, "Resilience in the face of potential trauma," *Current Directions in Psychological Science*, 14(3) (2005): 135–138.

18   A. S. Masten, "Ordinary magic: Resilience processes in development," *American Psychologist*, 56(3) (2001): 227.

our love of God. It is these everyday miracles that give us the strength to pass the tests, chosen for us specifically by our Creator, to elevate our soul like a spiritual banner for all of mankind.

Now, let us focus on the other condition of resilience.

SUCCESSFUL ADAPTATION DESPITE ADVERSE CIRCUMSTANCES

What is considered "successful adaptation" in the face of trauma or adversity? This question is debated among resilience researchers. Most define successful adaptation as having better than expected positive outcomes compared to others experiencing similar life circumstances. Of course, positive outcomes are not the "be all and end all" of a person's life. They are merely whatever behavior, characteristic, or accomplishment is most suitable for the age and circumstance of the participants, as well as convenient and interesting for the researchers in a particular study.

What is considered a successful outcome is often defined according to the values of society at large. For children, this includes getting good grades in school, being popular with their peers, and feeling confident. For adults, obtaining a university degree, having a professional career, receiving a high salary, and feeling a sense of life satisfaction are often considered signs of success.

The values of the secular world, however, are not necessarily Torah values. Rather than being motivated by material and physical attainments, Judaism focuses on the development of positive *middos* (character traits). Judaism, for example, highlights the importance of inner strength rather than physical prowess. Ben Zoma would say: "Who is strong? One who has control over his [evil] inclination."[19]

One example of inner strength is Yosef, the favorite son of Yaakov, who was thrown into a pit by his brothers. He was brought to Egypt and sold as a slave to Potiphar, the chief executioner of Pharaoh, who eventually appointed Yosef to be in charge of his entire household. Potiphar's wife noticed his handsomeness and tried to seduce him on several occasions. This was a tremendous test for Yosef, who had no

---

19   *Pirkei Avos* 4.

family ties in Egypt. In Egypt, which was infamous for immorality and licentiousness, it would have been natural for Yosef to simply "indulge." Potiphar's wife nearly succeeded in seducing Yosef until he saw the image of his father's face in his reflection from the window and resisted her overtures.

Potiphar placed Yosef in the royal jail. There, "God was with Yosef."[20] Pharaoh was angry with the head baker and the head butler and placed them in the same prison as Yosef. Our Sages tell us this was because a stone was found in the bread and a fly in a cup of wine. Both ministers had disturbing dreams on the very same night, and Yosef offered to interpret their dreams. The butler dreamed that he pressed three grapes into Pharaoh's cup and placed the cup in his palm. His dream demonstrated an active and passionate devotion to his role as Pharaoh's butler, so Yosef realized that he would be restored to his position.[21] The baker dreamed that three wicker baskets with bread were on his head and birds were eating from them. As the baker was a passive observer in his dream, Yosef saw that he did not deserve to be reinstated to his job.[22] Three days later, on Pharaoh's birthday, Yosef's interpretation was shown to be true. The butler was returned to his position, while the baker was hung as birds ate from his flesh.

Two years later, Pharaoh had two dreams and was not satisfied with any of his advisors' interpretations. The butler then told Pharaoh of Yosef's correct interpretation of his dream while in prison, so Pharaoh summoned Yosef. Our Sages teach us that Yosef's freedom came on Rosh Hashanah, when many prayers are answered. Pharaoh told Yosef of his dreams. In one dream, seven healthy cows were grazing. Suddenly, seven other cows emerged that were scrawny and emaciated. These inferior cows ate up the first seven healthy cows. In another dream, seven good ears of corn were eaten by seven withered, thin ears of corn. What

---

20   *Bereishis* 39.
21   Y. Frand, *Rabbi Yissocher Frand on the Haggadah* (New York: Mesorah Publications, 2018).
22   Ibid.

could not be explained was how there could be both good and bad at the same time.[23]

Yosef interpreted the dreams as revealing that there would be seven years of plenty in Egypt, followed by seven years of intense hunger. Yosef offered his advice to Pharaoh to appoint a wise person to gather and store the grain for seven years, to prepare for the years of hunger. This answered Pharaoh's question about both good and bad coexisting. During the first seven years, the second set of seven years of famine was already in existence, as they were preparing for it by collecting and storing the surplus grain. During the second set, the first set of seven years was still at their side, as they had the food from that period stored away.[28] Pharaoh appointed Yosef to the job, making Yosef the second most powerful person in Egypt after himself.

Pharaoh's dreams can be interpreted as symbolic of Yosef's own life, intermixed with challenging and prosperous periods. During the successful periods, Yosef was strengthening his *middos*, while in times of adversity, he was testing those *middos*. His rise from slave to viceroy might be considered the pinnacle of his success. However, this may not necessarily be considered his greatest success, or even perhaps one of *his* successes at all: We are told that his designation as a ruler of Egypt was orchestrated by God, Who gave Yosef Divine favor and wisdom as a way to bring forth the prophecy of the redemption of the Jewish People from slavery in Egypt.

What *is* extraordinary was Yosef's extreme faith and steadfast dedication to his true and unique purpose. Yosef retained his identity despite being submerged in an environment that was completely counter to Jewish values. Yosef was the first to leave his home and live in an alien culture.[24] Unlike Avraham, who lived on the outskirts of society, teaching morality to individuals, Yosef was second-in-command of the most powerful empire of his day. With such tremendous power came enormous responsibility and constant scrutiny. His biggest challenge

23   https://www.chabad.org/parshah/article_cdo/aid/557137/jewish/Why-did-Pharaoh-accept-Yosefs-dream-interpretations.htm.

24   Rabbi Ari Kahn, http://www.aish.com/tp/i/moha/48936522.html.

was his greatest success: He maintained his holiness and purity despite living in the spiritual void and being exposed to the material entice-ments of Egypt. This is his legacy, his spiritual banner for the genera-tions of our people to follow.

The story of Yosef highlights an important point about the definition of success. As our Jewish values often run counter to the barometer of achievement set in the outside world, someone who is considered extraordinary in the secular world may not necessarily register as being successful by Jewish standards and values. For example, we are taught that while we should be assured about our own unique identities, we should be modest in our achievements.

In our society today, humility is not highly celebrated. Our political leaders tout their skills and qualities in order to become elected. On so-cial media, those who are highly exhibitionist about their lives tend to be most popular. Yet, when we look at the leaders of our Jewish past, we find tremendous humility. For example, when Aharon was appointed as the first Kohen Gadol (high priest) at the Tabernacle's inauguration, he was hesitant to assume his duties because of his involvement in the Golden Calf. His brother, Moshe, came over to him and asked: "Why are you fearful? *L'kach nivcharta*—You were chosen for this!"[25] The Baal Shem Tov takes these two words, *l'kach nivcharta*, and delves further into their meaning.[26] According to the Baal Shem Tov, it was *because* Aharon was embarrassed and contrite about his error that he was chosen to be the Kohen Gadol. These qualities—humility and fear of God—create true leaders. The distinction between the secular and Torah perspective should be kept in mind when considering what we define as "successful adaptation" in the face of adversity.

DOES RESILIENCE LAST?

Resilience is a lifelong learning pursuit, not an absolute state of being. We may not show resilience continually, in every probable circumstance,

---

25   *Vayikra* 9:7 and *Rashi* ad loc.
26   Rabbi Levi Avtzon, https://www.chabad.org/parshah/article_cdo/aid/1167111/jewish/Afraid-Good.htm.

and in totality. Resilience is not a destination but a journey we take on a daily basis. Sometimes we may struggle and falter, especially when new circumstances present themselves. Each time we step outside our comfort zone and confront new challenges and complexities, however, we build our capacity for renewed resilience.

Resilient people are not invulnerable to pain, sadness, or suffering. For most of us, positive growth and distress coexist.[27] Often, when overcoming difficult circumstances, residual pain lies just below the surface. For example, losing a loved one can be compared to losing a limb. The pain of this loss will never cease. There are times when this anguish is felt more acutely than others, particularly at life-cycle events, such as graduations, weddings, and births.

Resilience is not about forgetting heartbreaks and dismissing sorrows but integrating these experiences into our new reality to create a sense of oneness. An active acceptance of, and cohesion with, our past allows us to move forward with our lives in the fullest sense. These trials have not broken us; they have helped form us into wiser and stronger people.

> Resilience is not about forgetting heartbreaks and dismissing sorrows but integrating these experiences into our new reality to create a sense of oneness.

We can also become more resilient as new strengths and opportunities present themselves in our lives. Later adolescence (around eighteen) in particular is a time when "late bloomers" may follow a more positive direction and get their lives on track.[28] This may be due to rapid brain development, resulting in better problem-solving and planning skills, and new life experiences, such as going to college, that occur during this period.[29]

As we settle into adulthood, further opportunities for resilience emerge. Turning points, such as marriage, the birth of our first child, joining the workforce, and becoming part of a community can set in

---

27   R. G. Tedeschi and L. Calhoun, "Post-traumatic growth: A new perspective on psychotrau-matology," *Psychiatric Times*, 21(4) (2004): 58–60.

28   A. S. Masten and A. J. Barnes, "Resilience in Children: Developmental Perspectives," *Children* (Basel, Switzerland), 5(7) (2018): 98.

29   Ibid.

motion a change in our life's direction, especially for those who experienced a challenging childhood and/or adolescence. A study spanning from childhood to adulthood, for example, found that the majority of troubled teens became responsible adults with stable families and jobs in their third and fourth decades of life.[30] As adults, individuals usually are able to move beyond their adverse childhood circumstances and establish a secure home life.

There are also those who remained steadfast and resilient, even when facing the most tremendous challenges. Some have lost everything in this world but did not waver in their hope and dedication. There are personal accounts of Holocaust survivors whose entire families perished, yet they managed not only to survive but to rebuild their lives.

Others, when faced with tragedy, were able to risk their own lives to save a life, which is commensurate with saving an entire world.[31] In 2008, a massacre occurred in Mumbai, India, where six people were brutally shot dead by terrorists, including Chabad rabbi Gavriel Holtzberg and his wife, Rivkah. Miraculously, their two-year-old son, Moshe, was saved. The nanny, Sandra Samuel, courageously reentered the upper floor of the Chabad house during the siege to rescue Moshe. This story of bravery challenges us to consider how we would respond when faced with such an unthinkable situation. Would we cower in fright or stand and fight for what we believe in, for what we love?

Despite the possibility of resilience, trauma and tragedy can lead to serious, long-lasting difficulties for many people.[32] Resilience in the face of catastrophe is challenging. Encouraging resilience should not come at the expense of empathy for those suffering in the midst and aftermath of tragedy.

---

30   E. Werner, "Resilience and recovery: Findings from the Kauai longitudinal study," *Research, Policy, and Practice in Children's Mental Health*, 19(1) (2005): 11–14.

31   Mishnah, *Sanhedrin* 4:5; *Talmud Yerushalmi* 4:9; *Talmud Bavli, Sanhedrin* 37a.

32   A. Sameroff, L. M. Gutman, and A. C. Peck, "Adaptation among youth facing multiple risks: Prospective research findings," *Resilience and vulnerability: Adaptation in the context of childhood adversities*, 1 (2003): 364–391.

RESILIENCE EXERCISE

Can we quantify resilience? As resilience varies according to the time, place, and situation, this is not a straightforward task. Researchers, however, have developed questionnaires that measure the positive attributes of a person and their environment, as a way of assessing their capacity for resilience. Here is an adaptation of one of these measurements, called the Connor-Davidson Resilience Scale,[33] which has been shown to be a valid and reliable measure of resilience for different groups of people. For the most part, these questions focus on personal strengths (with the exception of the second question). Answering these questions may be helpful in understanding your own personal strengths that would benefit from enhancement.

Respond to these questions based on how you felt over the past month. The total score ranges from 0–100 (the average score is around 80), with higher scores reflecting greater resilience over the past month.

	0 not true at all	**1** rarely true	**2** sometimes true	**3** often true	**4** true most of the time
I am able to adapt to change.					
I have close and secure relationships.					
When facing a challenging situation, I believe that God can help.					
I can deal with whatever comes my way.					

33   K. M. Connor and J. R. Davidson, "Development of a new resilience scale: The Connor-Davidson resilience scale (CD-RISC)," *Depression and anxiety*, 18(2) (2003): 76–82.

My past successes give me confidence to face new challenges.					
I try to see the humorous side of problems.					
I believe that coping with stressful situations strengthens me.					
I tend to recover well after illness or hardship.					
I believe that things happen for a reason.					
I give my best effort no matter what.					
I believe that I can achieve my goals despite facing obstacles.					
Even when things look hopeless, I don't give up.					
When I have a problem, I know where to turn for help.					
When I am under pressure, I can stay focused and think clearly.					
I prefer to take the lead in problem-solving.					

I am not easily discouraged by failure.					
I think of myself as a strong person.					
When necessary, I can make unpopular or difficult decisions.					
I can handle unpleasant feelings.					
When necessary, I can act on a hunch.					
I have a strong sense of purpose and meaning in life.					
I can control my responses to life situations.					
I like challenges.					
I work hard to attain my goals.					
I have pride in my achievements.					

Chapter Two

WHAT IS ADVERSITY?

On the pathway to resilience, we must first understand the nature and impact of adversity. While fostering resilience provides us with the necessary skills to bounce forward from life's challenges (both big and small), an understanding of adversity itself is an important part of our healing. We are better prepared to respond in ways that lessen its (potentially) negative impact on ourselves and our loved ones.

Resilience research refers to adversity as a risk factor since it increases our risk of poor outcomes.[1] Adversity can include catastrophic events, such as war and natural disasters; family traumas, such as bereavement and divorce; economic hardships, such as poverty and unemployment; health problems, such as physical and mental illness; and exposure to negative environments, such as dangerous neighborhoods.

Adversity represents those circumstances or events that are inherently difficult, both in their scope and effect, leading us to experience grief,

---

1   J. L. Johnson and J. E. Rolf, "When children change: Research perspectives on children of alcoholics," *Alcohol and the family: Research and clinical perspectives,*" (1990):162–193.

sadness, and sorrow. Adversity is uncontrollable and often unexpected. It disrupts our lives, making normal living extremely challenging and painful. It poses a fundamental threat to our basic human needs, including our physical sustenance and protection, emotional security and attachment, and social interaction and connection.

In almost all cases, adversity represents a loss of someone or something we cherished—the loss of a loved one, a loss of trust, the loss of stability and security, a loss of identity, or the loss of freedom. Some of these losses are tangible, such as when we are bereaved and can no longer spend time with a deceased loved one. Other losses are symbolic, such as the loss of trust between a husband and wife once manipulation and deceit have entered the marriage. Loss highlights our vulnerability and temporality. In a single second, our lives can be forever changed.

> Adversity represents a loss—the loss of a loved one, a loss of trust, the loss of stability and security, or the loss of freedom.

Judaism acknowledges the transient nature of our lives. During the holiday of Sukkos, we live in huts for seven days to remind us that this world is an interim dwelling place. At Pesach, we remember and appreciate our freedom, through reliving the bondage and liberation of our ancestors in Egypt. These holidays serve to connect us with our past as well as highlight our finite and fleeting presence in this world. We shift from place to place: from house to hut, from bondage to freedom, from suffering to salvation. Our lives unfold to reveal occasions of contentment, pleasure, and *simchah* (joy), alternating or coinciding with episodes that are bittersweet, disappointing, or mournful. As one door closes, another door opens.

On Sukkos, we read the book of *Koheles* (Ecclesiastes), which grapples with the philosophical meaning of life in light of its impermanence:

> *A season is set for everything, a time for every experience under heaven:*
> *A time for being born and a time for dying,*
> *A time for planting and a time for uprooting the planted;*
> *A time for slaying and a time for healing,*

A time for tearing down, a time for building up;

A time for weeping and a time for laughing,

A time for wailing and a time for dancing;

A time for throwing stones and a time for gathering stones,

A time for embracing and a time for shunning embraces;

A time for seeking and a time for losing,

A time for keeping and a time for discarding;

A time for ripping and a time for sewing,

A time for silence and a time for speaking;

A time for loving and a time for hating,

A time for war and a time for peace.[2]

Koheles, attributed to Shlomo HaMelech, laments that our downfall is not our transience but our futile attempt to deny this ultimate truth. Despite the meaninglessness of earthly pleasures, *Koheles* states that these should be enjoyed, as they are gifts from the hand of God. What is emphasized, though, is that these simple comforts are fleeting, while our mitzvos are eternal. The book concludes with the following injunction: "The sum of the matter, when all is said and done: Revere God and observe His commandments, for this applies to all mankind."[3]

There is no denying that adversity, along with the challenges, changes, and complexities that accompany it, often leads us to our own struggle with the meaning of life. At the same time, life's inevitable ebb and flow imbue within us an appreciation for what we might otherwise take for granted. Its impermanence reminds us that whatever we have in this world, whether in happiness or sorrow, is ours but for a passing moment, with the exception of our mitzvos and our relationship with God.

WHAT MIGHT BE OUR EMOTIONAL RESPONSES TO ADVERSITY?

Since adversity represents a loss in our lives, it is appropriate that we grieve. Grieving involves a confusing and unexpected cocktail of painful

---

2   *Koheles* 3:1–9.
3   Ibid., 12:13.

emotions. Yet, it is an important process in our recovery, enabling us to make sense of, and cope with, loss.

Research on grieving originally focused on bereavement. However, researchers soon realized that people also grieve when they experience other losses, such as divorce, illness, and even personal changes, such as moving or retirement. Grief is a normal response to any situation that requires an adjustment of our everyday assumptions. When we experience loss, our reality shifts and our emotions may become out of our control. As a result, many of us undergo a series of emotions that come and go throughout the grieving process.[4] For example, we might feel a sense of shock, confusion, exhaustion, denial, anger, guilt, shame, sadness, and fear.[5] It is important to keep in mind that the passage through grief is highly individualized, with each person experiencing a different set and timeline of emotional responses.

Shock is usually one of the first emotions to appear after a loss. Much of the confusion we experience in the immediate aftermath of trauma appears to result from threats to beloved assumptions of mastery, meaning, and self-worth.[6] When these assumptions are shattered, we often do not know how to respond. It is almost as though we walked into a new reality that cannot be recognized or understood. Depending on the significance of the traumatic event, we may experience a sense of shock and numbness for several days, or even weeks. This sense of confusion often accompanies a sense of utter exhaustion and depletion. The accomplishment of normal daily tasks can seem insurmountable. This exhaustion serves a purpose, however, forcing the grieved to obtain much-needed rest and recuperation.

Denial is another common emotion that occurs at the very beginning of a painful situation. Often, we live in a state of denial until our circumstances become too difficult to withstand any longer. We are

---

4   E. Kübler-Ross and D. Kessler, *On Grief and Grieving: Finding the Meaning of Grief through the Five Stages of Loss* (Simon and Schuster, 2005).

5   P. K. Maciejewski, B. Zhang, S. D. Block, and H. G. Prigerson, "An empirical examination of the stage theory of grief," *Jama*, 297(7) (2007): 716–723.

6   R. Janoff-Bulman, "Rebuilding shattered assumptions after traumatic life events," *Coping: The Psychology of What Works* (1999): 305–323.

creatures of habit: we crave stability, even when our life is unfulfilling and painful. Sometimes when we are faced with personal trauma, we deny that there is anything wrong. Denial often prolongs the very pain we are trying to avoid. In the face of tragedy, however, this time lag between the traumatic event and an understanding that our lives have permanently changed can serve as a defense mechanism that allows us to (more) gently adjust to the pain of our loss.

Anger also often appears when confronting tragedy. Anger encourages us to confront the reality of our new situation. Grieving individuals often feel a deep sense of fatigue, increased anxiety, and generalized helplessness. Anger mobilizes psychological resources for the grieving process, providing energy to cope with adversity.[7] Anger can therefore energize us to perform the actions necessary to establish equilibrium after a loss. However, excessive anger is not productive and can do us much harm. According to the Torah perspective, anger is a sign that someone is not aware that what is happening is God's will. For this reason, we must be careful not to allow anger to become part of our character. Rather, we must control our anger before it controls us. One possible way of controlling our anger is to acknowledge that there is not always a solution that fixes every situation. Although we often think that every problem has a solution, this fuels our frustration when we find out this is not always the case. The most productive attitude to bring to such a situation is not to focus on finding a solution but rather to concentrate on how to best face and handle the challenge at hand.[8]

Guilt and **shame** can also plague those who are grieving. While we can feel both guilt and shame at the same time, they are considered separate emotions.

- Guilt is a negative evaluation of one's actions, whether real or imagined. When something bad happens, we feel remorse over our behavior.

---

7   Tunajek, https://www.aana.com/docs/default-source/wellness-aana.com-web-documents-(all)/change-grief-and-healing.pdf?sfvrsn=a92c4bb1_2 (2009).

8   "Controlling anger before it controls you," American Psychological Association, https://www.apa.org/topics/anger/control.

- Shame, on the other hand, is a negative evaluation of one's self.[9] When experiencing negative life circumstances, shame involves feeling regret over some aspect of who we are as a person.

Both emotions encourage a balance between an individual's desires and the rights and needs of others.[10] Generally, guilt is considered to be more positive than shame. Guilt focuses on our behavior, while shame is focused upon fundamental aspects of our identity.[11] When one feels remorse over their actions and seeks forgiveness, guilt can be an important part of the healing process. Shame, on the other hand, is often fueled by feelings of being worthless and deeply flawed, which may lead to self-destructive behaviors. Brené Brown defines shame as "the intensely painful feeling or experience of believing we are flawed and therefore unworthy of connection and belonging."[12] Shame is more difficult to resolve than guilt, due to its internal nature, but may be relieved through self-compassion and nurturing our relationships with others.

Shame Resilience Theory (SRT), developed by Brené Brown, explores strategies to overcome feelings of shame.[13] SRT provides strategies that encourage feelings of empathy, connection, power, and freedom rather than shame. There are four steps to shame resilience.

1. Recognize and accept personal vulnerability. We are all vulnerable to feelings of shame. When we are able to recognize our emotional and physical signs of shame and understand what triggers our shame, we are able to move forward and seek help.
2. Raise critical awareness of social and contextual expectations. This is about understanding how expectations from

9   J. P. Tangney, J. Stuewig, and D. J. Mashek, "Moral emotions and moral behavior," *Annual Review of Psychology*, 58 (2007): 345–372.

10   C. Bastin, B. J. Harrison, C. G. Davey, J. Moll, and S. Whittle, "Feelings of shame, embarrassment and guilt and their neural correlates: A systematic review," *Neuroscience & Biobehavioral Reviews*, 71 (2016): 455–471.

11   S. M. Tignor and C. R. Colvin, "The interpersonal adaptiveness of dispositional guilt and shame: A meta-analytic investigation," *Journal of Personality*, 85(3) (2017): 341–363.

12   B. Brown, "Shame resilience theory: A grounded theory study on women and shame," *Families in Society*, 87(1) (2006): 43–52.

13   Ibid.

our environment and the larger society fuel our shame as individuals.

3. Connect with others to receive and offer empathy. This is about reaching out to others for support and recognizing that our most isolating experiences are universal. We recognize that we are not defective, rather our experiences and feelings are normal.

4. Discuss and deconstruct the feelings of shame. When we learn the language of shame and can draw distinctions among shame, guilt, embarrassment, and humiliation, we are able to separate shame from other emotions. We are able to ask for what we need and share what we know with others.

Self-blame can also set in as we struggle to make sense of our loss. Guilt and shame are both self-reflective emotions that involve self-blame, which is conceptualized as a cognitive state of attribution (when we think our actions caused our loss).[14] With self-blame, we wonder whether the outcome would change *if only* we had done something different. Research shows that self-blame can hinder the healthy progression of mourning, leading to post-traumatic symptoms, depression, and anxiety, particularly for bereaving parents.[15] Self-compassion may help to alleviate self-blame (see page 91).

According to Rabbi Lord Jonathan Sacks, "Judaism is a religion of hope, and its rituals of repentance and atonement are part of that hope."[16] As humans, we are prone to making mistakes, not only through our failings but sometimes through our inability to know the best course to follow. In the Jewish perspective, we should acknowledge our limitations and misjudgments of the past while focusing on how we can improve and better ourselves in the present and future. While it is important to accept our role in the situation, forgiving ourselves is essential to moving forward. In many instances, there is nothing that

---

14   R. Janoff-Bulman, "Characterological versus behavioral self-blame: Inquiries into depression and rape," *Journal of Personality and Social Psychology*, 37(10) (1979): 1798.

15   C. Duncan and J. Cacciatore, "A systematic review of the peer-reviewed literature on self-blame, guilt, and shame," *OMEGA-Journal of Death and Dying*, 71(4) (2015): 312–342.

16   "The Scapegoat: Shame and Guilt," https://rabbisacks.org/the-scapegoat-shame-and-guilt-achrei-mot-kedoshim-5775/.

we could have done differently to change the nature of the outcome. We have to recognize which situations require a rethinking of our lives—how we might improve ourselves in order to avoid making similar mistakes in the future—and which situations are completely beyond our control. For example, most divorced people eventually develop an understanding of their role in the dissolution of their marriage and can reflect on how they have changed as a result. On the other hand, there are tragedies where we have little or no control, which are completely in God's hands. In the initial stages of such a tragedy, however, our perspective is not likely to be realistic and objective, and we often require support and guidance for recovery.

Sadness is the most typical emotion that accompanies grieving. Sadness allows us to truly feel what we have lost. However, sadness, like anger, has its negative aspects. Prolonged sadness may lead to a downward spiral, in which a low mood and the negative thoughts that often accompany sadness influence one other reciprocally, leading to a worsening state and even clinical depression.[17] Particularly detrimental is focusing passively on the negative emotions that may follow adversity for a prolonged period of time.[18]

According to the Jewish perspective, we must try to overcome our sadness, as it impedes our spiritual progress. Clearly, there are times when sadness is appropriate.[19] We are obligated to feel sad when someone dies, for example. We are also taught to empathize with another person's suffering.

Chassidic teaching differentiates between two types of sadness:[20] *merirus*, which is constructive grief, and *atzvus*, which is destructive grief. *Merirus* is the distress of someone who recognizes their failings

---

17   A. T. Beck (Ed.), *Cognitive Therapy of Depression* (Guilford press,1979); C. Peterson and M. E. Seligman, "Causal explanations as a risk factor for depression: Theory and evidence," *Psychological review*, 91(3) (1984): 347.

18   S. Nolen-Hoeksema, L. E. Parker, and J. Larson, "Ruminative coping with depressed mood following loss," *Journal of Personality and Social Psychology*, 67(1) (1994): 92.

19   *Tanya*, chap. 27 in E. Dessler, *Strive for the Truth! Part 2*, trans. A. Carmell (Jerusalem: Feldheim, 1978).

20   Y. Tauber, https://www.chabad.org/library/article_cdo/aid/144578/jewish/Good-Grief.htm.

and wants to improve, while *atzvus* is the despair of someone whose sadness results in feelings of hopelessness and apathy. These two types of sadness lead to very different outcomes when the mourning passes:

- When we experience *merirus*, we make important changes in response to our sadness—reflecting, resolving, and reforming in order to work through the causes of our sorrow.
- When we experience *atzvus*, on the other hand, we might give up.

Sadness that leads to despair and depression is destructive. However, when sadness is limited and controlled, it can be a powerful tool for spiritual progress.[21] This teaches us that sadness, when we restrain and direct it, can serve a higher purpose. It can help us to appreciate life and prompt us to make the necessary changes that promote healing.

Fear can also accompany loss, particularly when the loss is sudden and tragic. In response, the grieved might become fearful of the seemingly precarious nature of life. Being overly cautious often provides us with a sense of control over the uncontrollable. While fear offers some initial comfort through providing an illusion of control, it can also be extremely debilitating when someone limits their life. On the other hand, the experience of loss can motivate us to challenge our fears. Once we have faced the unimaginable, we may be able to push past our limitations to accomplish more than we ever previously considered possible.

In Hebrew, the word *yirah* means "to fear," which is related to the word *raah*, meaning "to see."[22] The concept of *yirah* teaches us that life's essential choice is whether to open our eyes in wonder, experiencing the full spectrum of possibilities, or close our eyes in avoidance, having a meaningless, dull existence. In Judaism, one of our primary obligations is to fear God. We fulfill this mitzvah (commandment) through our careful observance of the Torah and understanding that God knows and sees everything. Such awareness motivates us to achieve our potential by maximizing our time here in this world. However, sometimes

---

21 E. E. Dessler, *Strive for the Truth! Part 4: Sanctuaries in Time*, trans. A. Carmell (Jerusalem: Feldheim, 2002).

22 A. Fertig, *Bridging the Gap: Clarifying the Eternal Foundations of Mussar and Emunah for Today*, (Jerusalem: Feldheim, 2007).

we blind ourselves to reality, burying our heads in the sand with the illusion of comfort. Through the pain of loss, however, we may awaken from this slumber. In awareness of this Heavenly fear, we realize the importance of our actions, understanding that all fears are insignificant compared to the fear of God.[23]

Many psychologists have noted that the grieving process can eventually lead to recovery and resilience. Depending on the circumstances, there is great diversity in one's path through grief. Experts suggest that grieving may last from several months to one or two years.[24] In some instances, grieving may continue for ten to twenty years or even a lifetime. Grief-work and therapy may be helpful for some individuals who experience prolonged grieving. For those who are experiencing healthy grieving, on the other hand, there are indications that therapies and interventions may be ineffective, or even deleterious.[25] Most counselors agree that we should allow ourselves time to mourn, noting that healthy grieving is the most common reaction to a significant loss. Healthy grieving means that we integrate our loss into our life, move forward, and adjust to a life that begins anew.[26]

> Healthy grieving means that we integrate our loss into our life, move forward, and adjust to a life that begins anew.

HOW CAN WE LESSEN THE IMPACT OF TRAUMATIC CIRCUMSTANCES?

While traumatic events take their toll, the evidence suggests that the effects of isolated setbacks tend to be rather modest.[27] Short-term stresses such as moving home, job loss, or acute illness are not likely

---

23   Ibid.

24   S. Zisook, M. Paulus, S. R. Shuchter, and L. L. Judd, "The many faces of depression following spousal bereavement," *Journal of Affective Disorders*, 45(1–2) (1997): 85–95.

25   R. A. Neimeyer, "Searching for the meaning of meaning: Grief therapy and the process of reconstruction," *Death studies*, 24(6) (2000): 541–558.

26   Tunajek, https://www.aana.com/docs/default-source/wellness-aana.com-web-documents-(all)/change-grief-and-healing.pdf?sfvrsn=a92c4bb1_2.

27   A. Sameroff, L. M. Gutman, and S. C. Peck, "Adaptation among youth facing multiple risks: Prospective research findings," *Resilience and Vulnerability: Adaptation in the Context of Childhood Adversities*, 1 (2003): 364–391.

to have long-term effects. Rather, small-scale difficulties teach us the coping skills we need when faced with bigger problems.[28]

One unfortunate aspect of life difficulties, however, is that they usually do not happen in isolation. Many negative situations tend to co-occur, as they have the same origin. Children who live in poverty, for instance, are more likely to live in poor neighborhoods, go to schools with fewer resources, and have exposure to environmental pollutants.

One hardship also often leads to another. Divorce, for example, not only involves the permanent separation of family, but also a decline in income for both parents, along with a move of address, which then brings the possibility of social isolation from close family and friends, and so on.

Dealing with numerous challenges is the norm, not the exception. We need to look no further than our ancient texts, which are replete with the struggles of our ancestors, with a non-exhaustive list that includes difficult childhoods, poor relationships with parents and siblings, unloving marriages, fertility problems, kidnapping, slavery, death threats, and abuse. A good example is Sarah Imeinu, who had to wait ninety years to conceive her only child, Yitzchak—in addition to being kidnapped (twice!). According to the midrash, Satan told Sarah that Avraham took Yitzchak to Mount Moriah and slaughtered him, offering him up on the altar as a sacrifice.[29] Sarah began to cry, moaning, and her soul departed from her body. Avraham came from Mount Moriah to discover that she had died.

As one might expect, there is an inverse relationship between adversity and positive functioning. As the number of life challenges increases, the likelihood of positive adjustment decreases. In one study, for example, researchers examined the impact of eight adverse family events during the first year of a child's life.[30] The events included: the death of a family member, the serious injury of a family member, a negative

---

28   E. Kübler-Ross and D. Kessler, *On Grief and Grieving: Finding the Meaning of Grief through the Five Stages of Loss* (Simon and Schuster, 2005).

29   Pirkei D'Rabbi Eliezer, chap. 31.

30   E. Flouri and N. Tzavidis, "Psychopathology and prosocial behavior in adolescents from socio-economically disadvantaged families: The role of proximal and distal adverse life events," *European Child & Adolescent Psychiatry*, 17 (2008): 498–506.

change in the parents' financial situation, a family member suffering from a mental/emotional problem, a move, the birth of a sibling, the imprisonment of a parent in jail, and the separation of parents. Their findings revealed that none of the eight family events in isolation predicted children's emotional and behavioral difficulties at a later point in time. Instead, it was the number rather than the type of event that predicted children's difficulties. The more events children experienced, the worse their outcomes three years later.

While it is easier said than done, reducing the negative impact of an adverse event and preventing further trauma are crucial to recovery. For children, it is particularly important to have the time and space to cope with the situation at hand. Here are strategies that have been found to help while on the road to recovery.[31]

- **Accept the process:** Appreciate that everyone needs time to grieve in their own healthy way, and there is no schedule that works for everyone.
- **Acknowledge vulnerability:** Understand that our defenses are usually down when suffering, and you may be particularly vulnerable, so be protective.
- **Move toward your goals:** Work on small goals and focus on specific tasks that can move you in the right direction.
- **Understand that recovery will happen:** Recognize that, while you may move back a few steps here and there, you are making progress.
- **Rely on friends and family:** It is important that you let your family and friends know what you need, whether it is emotional or practical support.
- **Step back from negativity:** Reduce your exposure to negative thoughts, people, and situations that impede your recovery.

31   R. A. Haine, T. S. Ayers, I. N. Sandler, and S. A. Wolchik, "Evidence-based practices for parentally bereaved children and their families," *Professional Psychology: Research and Practice*, 39(2) (2008): 113; J. Hawthorne, J. Jessop, J. Pryor, and M. Richards, *Supporting Children Through Family Change: A Review of Interventions and Services for Children of Divorcing and Separating Parents* (York: York Publishing, 2003); American Psychological Association (n.d.), "The road to resilience," retrieved from http://www.apa.org/helpcenter/road-resilience.aspx.

- **Limit change:** During stressful times, there is enough upheaval, so restrict any further changes to what is completely necessary.
- **Practice self-care:** Do practices that help you feel nurtured and at peace, but only those that are healthy both physically and emotionally in the long run.
- **Find a mantra:** Words can be healing. Find a specific saying or song that you can recite or sing whenever you feel stressed or worried, perhaps a prayer or hymn.
- **Consider other ways to aid recovery:** Journaling, meditation, volunteering, and positive visualization may also promote healing.
- **Seek professional help when needed:** If you are feeling as though you cannot cope, then seek professional help as soon as possible.
- **Pray to God:** Last but not least, remember to ask God for help on your pathway to recovery.

CLOSED DOORS, OPEN DOORS EXERCISE

"When one door closes, another opens; but we often look so long and so regretfully upon the closed door that we do not see the one which has opened for us."

Attributed to Alexander Graham Bell

"All beginnings require that you unlock new doors."

Rebbe Nachman of Breslov[32]

An ending marks the beginning of something new. This exercise is adapted from Martin Seligman, who is considered the father of positive psychology.[33] It can help us shift from focusing on what we have lost to seeing the potential of what can be gained. It can also help us to understand what is preventing our healing when a door closes.

---

32   M. Mykoff, *Empty Chair: Finding Hope and Joy—Timeless Wisdom from a Hasidic Master, Rebbe Nachman of Breslov* (Jewish Lights Publishing, 1994).

33   T. Rashid and M. Seligman, *Positive Psychotherapy: Workbook* (Oxford University Press, 2018).

First, think back to a time when a door closed, such as through a missed opportunity, a change in life circumstances, or the loss of a loved one. Now think about what happened after this door closed. What would have never happened if this first door had remained open? Write down these experiences (as many as possible that come to mind).

- The door that closed on me was:

  _____

- The new door that opened for me was:

  _____

Now, consider your experiences and answer the following questions:

- What preceded the door closing?
- What were the effects of the closed door? Did they last long?
- What helped you realize that a new door was open?
- How long did it take you to see that a new door was open?
- What stopped you from noticing the new open door?
- What does that closed door represent to you now?
- What did you learn?
- Which people helped you?
- What strategies helped you?
- What was unhelpful?
- What could you do to help yourself in the future?
- How could you help others?

Now, reflect on a new situation. Given your previous answers:

- How can you apply what you have learned to help you now?
- What people can you rely on to help you now?
- What strategies might be helpful in this situation?
- What might you avoid in this situation?

Chapter Three

WHAT ARE THE MAJOR LIFE CHALLENGES FACING US TODAY?

This chapter provides research findings and Torah insights on difficult circumstances that we may face in our lifetimes, including divorce, bereavement, mental and physical health problems, and child maltreatment. Each of these examples of hardships begins with a personal story from someone who has experienced that particular test. These are true stories from different individuals, who have offered to share their private struggles, misfortunes, and triumphs with the aim of helping others in similar situations. The personal narrative of divorce is my own; the others are anonymous.

Overall, this section was the most challenging to write, given the seriousness of its content, as well as the sensitivity that these significant challenges both demand and deserve. Likewise, because it is so "real," it is not an easy read, and some may choose to move on to the next chapter on fostering resilience. Nevertheless, this chapter's purpose is to convey information, as well as provide a sense of empathy for those who have experienced similar situations. What must be emphasized, however, is that each of us has our own unique life stories. Most research, in contrast, is based on an average of many individuals. As a result, research can only provide an impersonal understanding and overview of each adversity, in terms of its prevalence, related factors, typical responses, and possible outcomes, but the findings cannot, nor are they meant to, dictate or predict how any one particular situation will turn out.

It must also be noted that this section is not intended to be exhaustive, both in the overview of research on each adversity as well as the different challenges that we may experience. An understanding of each of these constitutes volumes, both in the breadth and depth of the experience itself as well as the research and professional advice that are available. Sadly, there are many more hardships—including those that are considered systemic, such as racism, poverty, unemployment, and poor schooling, as well as those that are often associated with other stresses, including substance abuse, eating disorders, self-harm, and attempted suicide—that require immediate professional help.

DIVORCE

Almost no one gets married with the possibility of divorce in their mind. This was especially true for me. My parents were divorced when I was quite young, and I wanted to avoid that experience for my own children. When I got married, I was determined that "this was it."

Still, life does not necessarily work out as you planned. After eight years of marriage and two children, he told me that he no longer loved me. He wanted a divorce. I was in complete shock. We had our difficulties, but I never expected this to happen. My grief was compounded by the news that my sister was diagnosed with breast cancer. Of course, these two events were unrelated, but they happened at the same time. I felt completely vulnerable with the potential simultaneous loss of both my marriage and my sister. It was as though my outer layer, which protected me from the elements, was stripped away. I felt everything so acutely and deeply, which might have been a blessing in some respects. The fragility and temporality of this world were no longer abstract to me. This realization remains with me to this day—and has, in many ways, become a friend that has taught me to live my life as it is meant to be lived.

Over the next year, the shared lives of our family unraveled, raveled, and then unraveled again. I was in a state of denial and not ready to accept that I would be a divorced mother with young children. I felt very ashamed. I did whatever I could to prevent the divorce. Nothing worked and, in the process, I lost my sense of self-worth and self-respect.

Nearly a year later, I accepted that change was inevitable. I remember the day when I finally realized that this was meant to be. I was taking a walk in the park and the sun was shining brightly. I had a "lightbulb" moment. It became crystal clear to me that, somewhere along the line, I had stopped living for myself. That the love I was giving was not being received. That I could no longer be in a marriage where I did not recognize myself. That I deserved to be loved.

I received a get (Jewish divorce), and I felt as though my life with the man who had been my husband was severed in two.

Many changes happened very quickly. Thank God, these changes were positive ones. I rented a house with my children almost next door to my best friends' and near my children's school. My dear babysitter became our nanny—and a lifesaver. I was offered my dream job. My friendship circle became larger, and my friends within that circle dearer to me. God was present in every moment of every day, making sure that I had what I needed and constantly reminding me of His love.

Understanding the precariousness of life, I was determined that I would no longer make decisions based on shame and fear. I would fully experience and engage in my life, even if it meant that sometimes I would feel pain. This required putting myself "out there." Saying yes when I was invited out for Shabbos lunch to people's houses. Saying yes to attending single events and shiurim as much as possible.

My rebbetzin used to say to me, "You never know what is around the corner." She was right. Thank God, within a year of my divorce, I married again, and my husband and I are blessed with several children.

Looking back, this was such a challenging time in my life and, even now, I have tears in my eyes as I write my story. But I know that this is what needed to happen. I am so thankful for my life, my husband, my children, and my sister's continued good health. Through the experience of this loss, I found myself. I discovered who I am, what I am capable of, and what is important to me. This understanding has given me the strength to live my life to the fullest, married to my true zivug (life partner).

Divorce is one of the most stressful yet common experiences in modern life. Since the 1970s, there has been an upward trend in divorce rates globally, although this varies from country to country.[1]

In the US, almost 50 percent of the couples who marry obtain a divorce at a later point in time. In the UK, there is a growing trend for break-ups in longer-established marriages. In Tokyo, divorce ceremonies have become a popular ritual where couples invite family and friends to celebrate the end of their marriage. Recent reports suggest that divorce rates are also rising for the Orthodox community.[2]

There are many possible reasons to explain why divorce rates have increased since the 1970s:

- Divorce is more socially acceptable and carries less stigmatization than in the past.
- Legal and religious reforms have made divorce easier to obtain.
- Society has become more individualistic, leading to a greater focus on oneself and the fulfillment of one's individual desires.
- In our "have it all" society, we often develop unrealistic expectations about marriage, expecting our spouses to make us complete and happy at all times.
- There is less contact and cohesion in the wider family and community, which puts greater pressure on the nuclear family.
- The internet offers people an easy way to find past loves, visit social websites, and meet possible partners.

Whatever the reasons, divorce is a painful, difficult, and life-changing process. Divorce is a physical and psychological separation, which has

---

1   Esteban Ortiz-Ospina and Max Roser, "Marriages and Divorces" (2020), OurWorldInData. org. Retrieved from: https://ourworldindata.org/marriages-and-divorces.

2   Https://www.timesofisrael.com/jewish-divorces-in-israel-up-5-in-2018-with-86-increase-in-one-central-town/.

both practical and emotional ramifications. Practically, divorce involves a complete rupture between the shared lives of two people. This is an unsettling process that requires a reorganization of one's life. All material possessions are divided. Someone must move out of the family home. If there are children involved, children's residence and visitation need to be negotiated. A legal divorce must be obtained.

These stressful decisions are compounded by the emotional aspects of divorce. In the midst of coping with the practical considerations of divorce, one must also deal with the sense of mourning that accompanies it. Divorce represents a loss of shared hopes and dreams with another person. It is a loss of identity, resulting in a sense of uncertainty about one's present and future. Divorce can also bring on feelings of shame, as a visible sign to the outside world that one is fallible. As a result, a person is often left feeling unstable, rejected, and fragile.

For most people, resolution from divorce is extremely difficult. In many ways, divorce feels like a death. Following the death of a marriage, similar to bereavement, come sadness and pain. Unlike death, however, divorce does not provide a sense of closure. With a divorce, we have to acknowledge that the other person still exists but does not share our lives anymore. Closure can be especially difficult to achieve when children are involved, as a divorced couple share the bond of parenting. Painful, unresolved issues can continue to fester when one has to see their ex-spouse regularly for visitation as well as to communicate about decisions regarding children. Not surprisingly, it is often challenging to reorganize memories in the aftermath of divorce in a redemptive way. Nevertheless, divorce can provide great opportunities for personal growth and transformation.[3]

In the Jewish view, divorce is considered a spiritual amputation—a tragedy that sometimes is a necessity. When a Jewish couple marries according to Jewish law, their souls become one. Their destinies are united and their purpose in this world intertwined. As the Torah says,

---

3   E. M. Hetherington and J. Kelly, *For Better or For Worse: Divorce Reconsidered* (WW Norton & Company, 2002).

a married couple "becomes one flesh."[4] When a marriage becomes a diseased limb—threatening the life of the entire body—a person is left with the painful choice of spiritual death or amputation. In these cases, when there is no other solution possible, divorce is sanctioned by a *beis din* (Jewish court). A *get* terminates the marriage and allows the couple to remarry within Jewish law. Without a proper *get*, a Jewish couple remains legally and metaphysically bound together.

Divorce is like our exodus from Egypt.[5] Once freed, the Jewish nation followed Moshe in the desert, discovering their true Beloved at Mount Sinai. Similarly, a divorce, in these instances, represents liberation, providing redemption from an enslaved existence and opening up the possibility of finding one's true soul mate. Nevertheless, divorce is only considered as a final resort, when all other options have been attempted and failed. The Talmud says that when a divorce occurs, the Temple altar—the symbol of Jewish unity and holiness—metaphorically weeps as if to mourn the loss of this unsuccessful union.[6]

When divorce is necessary, however, there is no reason that the couple should harbor anger toward each other or toward God.[7] The experience may be required to bring about a certain stage of the rectification of one's soul or as a way of achieving some other aspect of God's plan for the world. If children are involved, then the purpose of their marriage may have been to bring these souls into the world. In other words, while tragic, when divorce is indeed essential, it can be considered part of our growth process, a step toward achieving our higher purpose.

Research also dispels the notion that divorce is merely a static event, which produces intense but temporary difficulties. Rather, marital disruption and failure represent a series of interconnected stages that comprise experiences leading to, and issuing from, divorce.[8] Couples

---

4   *Bereishis* 2:24.
5   See Chassidic commentary *Ramasayim Tzofim* on the beginning of *Tanna D'Vei Eliyahu Rabbah*, as described in Y. Ginsburgh, *Mystery of Marriage* (Jerusalem: Linda Pinsky Publications, 1999).
6   *Sanhedrin* 22a.
7   Ginsburgh, *Mystery of Marriage*.
8   Hetherington and Kelly, *For Better or For Worse*.

who divorce often experienced numerous difficulties throughout their marriage, and divorce is one of the consequences. Furthermore, the quality of life post-divorce is often a product of the past marriage, in addition to the decisions people make during their marital dissolution and in their subsequent lives. As a result, there are many diverse pathways from divorce, the consequences of which can be devastating as well as positive and life-transforming, for both adults and children.

For adults, the most problematic time is usually during the first and second years following a divorce. This is a time of resolution, reorganization, and restructuring. Given the multitude of decisions and changes involved, a recently divorced person often feels emotionally drained and physically exhausted. It is not surprising that studies following adults in the first few years after divorce find that they are more likely to suffer from disruptions to their well-being than people who are married.[9]

The repercussions of decision-making about education, work, children, family, friends, and new partners in these first few years after divorce may last a lifetime.[10] During this time, it is especially important to

- choose living situations that provide access to friends and family;
- maintain children's friendships and avoid school changes;
- establish positive patterns of parenting and family life;
- build a possible career path;
- set future goals and priorities (rather than dwell on past events);
- capitalize on strengths and available resources.

A study following divorced adults for twenty years found that those who planned for the future and made good decisions in the first few years after divorce were more likely to settle into a constructive path than those who were muddling through.[11] A substantial number of women, in particular, experienced personal and professional growth, success in parenthood, and often new marriages in the years to come. These women experienced self-discovery, fulfillment, and enhancement

---

9   P. R. Amato, "The consequences of divorce for adults and children," *Journal of Marriage and Family*, 62(4) (2000): 1269–1287.
10 Hetherington and Kelly, *For Better or For Worse*.
11 Ibid.

in their lives because they were able to access competencies that would have likely remained latent had they stayed in their marriages. Twenty years post-divorce, though, almost everyone in the study managed to cope reasonably well and their divorce was merely a "shadowy memory and one largely irrelevant to their current lives."

Children of divorced parents, however, may have a more difficult time. In general, parental divorce increases the risk of problems in childhood, adolescence, and even adulthood.[12] However, the problems associated with divorce for children vary greatly. Parental divorce is more difficult for some children than for others. Circumstances that make divorce more difficult for children include the following:

- Changes such as moving to a new home, living in a different neighborhood, and transferring schools, resulting in the loss of friendships and social circles.
- Less contact with the non-residential parent. When children have frequent, positive involvement from the non-custodial parent, research shows that children of divorced parents experience fewer problems and better adjustment.[13]
- Continued bickering between parents, especially through children, perpetuating the cycle of conflict that may have existed before the divorce and increasing the likelihood of additional stress.
- Less economic stability, as single parents usually have a lower income following divorce.[14]
- New romantic partners and the possibility of remarriage and stepsiblings, creating further disruption. This can be especially challenging for children when there are multiple remarriages.[15]

---

12   Ibid.

13   P. R. Amato, C. Dorius, and M. Lamb, "Fathers, children and divorce," in *The Role of the Father in Child Development*, 5 (2010), 177–200.

14   S. S. McLanahan, "Father absence and the welfare of children," in *Coping with Divorce, Single Parenting, and Remarriage: A Risk and Resiliency Perspective* (1999), 117–145.

15   E. M. Hetherington and A. M. Elmore, "Risk and resilience in children coping with their parents' divorce and remarriage," in *Resilience and Vulnerability: Adaptation in the context of Childhood Adversities* (2003), 182–212.

Many of the problems associated with divorce are often present in families long before the divorce occurs.[16] While divorce and remarriage usually contribute to a disruption in family life, such difficulties are usually temporary as long as the changes associated with it are largely positive. Most important is maximizing a sense of stability, loving and engaged parenting, frequent contact from the non-custodial parent, and cooperative co-parenting. For most children with divorced parents, resilience is the normative outcome. Studies following children with divorced parents into adulthood find that the vast majority (75 to 80 percent) develop into competent, well-adjusted adults.[17]

BEREAVEMENT

I am telling this story because I believe that whatever one goes through in life is given to us for a reason and that personal growth is sometimes achieved through our most difficult life experiences. One of the reasons I feel this took place was to acquire the necessary tools needed to help others in similar situations in the future.

Just over twenty years ago, during the summer holidays, we were expecting our ninth child. I had been through pregnancy quite a few times and thought I knew what to expect. Medically, everything seemed fine. In all of my pregnancies, my husband and I opted out of ultrasound scans, following the school of thought that if the doctors felt all seemed right, there was no need to look for problems.

The doctors did not have any concerns at all. The baby was growing well, the vital signs were there, and every check-up was routine. I, however, felt that this time, something was different. There was no pain or problem, just an innate, deeper sensation that made me feel sad a lot of the time and that there was something unusual about this pregnancy.

About a month before my due date, I experienced heavy discharges that concerned me. I asked the doctor several times, and he couldn't find an

---

16   Hetherington and Kelly, *For Better or For Worse*.

17   C. Ahrons, "Long-term effects of divorce on children," *Family Therapy Magazine* (2006): 24–27.

explanation. He decided to send me to the hospital to check it out. This was three weeks before the anticipated birth.

They checked me over, but not reaching any conclusion, they asked me to stay overnight for monitoring.

At this point, I want to mention two things: (1) These were the days before cell phones, and (2) I had never delivered a baby early; if anything, I was sometimes late.

So, my husband went home that afternoon to look after our younger children—our older three were in camp—and he told me he would come sometime the following morning to pick me up.

I went to sleep in the ward. A few hours later, I woke up with painful contractions. I called a nurse to let her know that I thought I was in labor. She didn't take me seriously. The contractions worsened. I think the nurse saw the contorted look on my face and felt sorry for me. They wheeled me down to the delivery room. I was alone with the midwives and nurses but wanted my husband there. It was the middle of the night; he was with my children and he probably would not answer the phone.

In the early hours of the morning, I gave birth. The staff looked solemn and didn't interact with me in a normal way. The baby wasn't crying. I was extremely uncomfortable, but everyone was busy with the baby.

I started praying. Please God, make everything okay. After what seemed like an eternity, someone told me that it was a boy, but that something was wrong. I asked for a phone to call my husband. The time was approximately 5:00 a.m. The phone line was busy. I tried countless times to no avail. I realized that one of the children must have knocked a phone off the hook. At 6:00 a.m., I phoned my neighbor and asked her to run over to my house to tell my husband to call the hospital.

He did, and I remember telling him, "We have good news and bad news. I gave birth to a baby boy, but something is wrong." He dropped the kids at the neighbor and rushed to join me at the hospital. It was a relief to have my husband with me, but I was in a state of shock, confusion, and fear.

They had taken an almost lifeless baby and tried valiantly to resuscitate him. I went with my husband to see him, and he looked like a pure angel. Three hours later, he returned his pure soul to his Maker.

He had a rare condition called Potter's syndrome; he was born without kidneys and could not survive outside of the womb. I was deeply grateful that an innocuous reason had brought me to the hospital. Had I delivered at home, I may never have known the reason for the baby's demise and would have blamed myself.

On that day, my husband arranged for the baby to have his bris. We named him Yisroel and the chevra kadisha buried him as a Jew.

I now had to pick up the pieces. I was offered therapy but preferred to work it out in my own way.

I strongly believe that Yisroel's soul had to come into this world to complete an unfinished task from a previous reincarnation. I had the huge privilege of carrying within me a soul of such beauty and holiness for close to nine months. He was never meant to grow up in this world but rather enter our space and life for a limited time. That belief gave me the strength and ability to carry on and take care of my other children.

I feel his presence in my life all the time. I don't talk about him, but I talk to him.

I often ask him to help me in different circumstances by acting as my messenger when I pray and speak to God on behalf of our family. He, a pure and holy soul, can achieve great things—and we are connected. To me, that is a great honor. It is a tremendous constant source of comfort to me.

We don't understand God's ways. However, we can learn lessons from everything He does in this world and build positivity through it.

Every year on his yahrzeit, I light a candle and recite the entire book of Tehillim so that I can reconnect to his holy soul and renew my strength and faith. It is a very private time but extremely meaningful and anchoring for me.

In life, one grows from one's challenges. I know I have, and I hope I can enable, in some small way, others to do the same.

May his memory be blessed.

Almost all of us will confront the loss of a loved one at some point in our lives. Death is inevitable. Still, the loss of a loved one is heartbreaking and can bring intense suffering as well as emotional and physical difficulties. When we lose someone we love, we lose a piece of ourselves. The closer our relationship, the more of ourselves we feel we have lost.

The bereaved not only have to cope with the loss of love and support, but they also have to learn how to redefine themselves in a world without their loved one. When death is tragic and unexpected, the bereaved suffer immense pain and confusion—a feeling of complete disorientation and disillusionment over the sudden loss. Even when death comes naturally at an older age, the loss of a loved one represents a redefinition and rethinking of one's purpose and role in life. Whatever the circumstances, bereavement brings the tragic loss of a loved one from our life in this world, which cannot be replaced.

Judaism, however, does not view death as a perpetual ending. Each living individual is the integration of body and soul. The body represents a temporary vehicle to imbue holiness in this world by the fulfillment of mitzvos, while the soul represents our true eternal self. A fundamental belief in Judaism is that life does not begin with birth and end with death. Rather, our soul existed before birth as a spiritual entity and continues to exist after the death of our physical body. The time in which our soul inhabits the physical body is just one phase of existence. Death is the separation of the body and soul, representing the dissolution of the body when the soul passes to a higher, exclusively spiritual existence in Gan Eden.

Jewish belief in the eternal soul may provide comfort to the bereaved. Nevertheless, this understanding does not diminish the emotional pain and sadness surrounding their physical absence in our everyday lives. The grief associated with bereavement can be one of the most profound of all human emotions—as well as one of the most distressing to endure.[18] A period of grief is a normal, healthy reaction to the loss of a loved one. The length and intensity of mourning, however, can vary greatly depending on the nature of the relationship with the person whom we have lost.

The death of a child, in particular, has more complicated and intense reactions of grief than any other type of bereavement. The loss of a child is an unfathomable tragedy, disrupting the natural law and order

---

18   B. Noel and P. D. Blair, *I Wasn't Ready to Say Goodbye: Surviving, Coping and Healing after the Sudden Death of a Loved One* (Sourcebooks, Inc., 2008).

of life. As parents, we expect that our children will outlive us, carrying forth our lineage into future generations. When parents lose a child, they can also lose hope for the future. Parents often feel tremendous guilt with the loss of a child. Parental responsibility involves nurturing, providing for, and protecting their children. When a child dies, parents can be left feeling as though they failed in their parental duties.

The suffering of bereaved parents is further complicated by the difficulties the loss of a child can establish within a marriage. As both parents are grieving for the loss of their child, they are often not able to provide support to each other. There may also be differences in the way each parent copes with their loss, which further complicates matters. Bereaved mothers tend to rely on emotive ways of coping such as discussing their feelings and seeking emotional support, while bereaved fathers often use avoidance as a means of coping, such as withdrawing and escapism.[19] Most tragically, the death of a child brings a heartbreak for which there is no substitute or replacement. The shock and severity surrounding the loss leaves parents feeling helpless and despairing, and this can last for many, many years—or even a lifetime.[20]

The loss of a spouse is generally considered one of the most stressful life events that one can experience in adulthood. A spouse is one's best friend and partner. A person's identity largely centers on his or her relationship with their spouse. With a spouse, one forms and shares a family, a circle of friends, their daily life patterns, and their hopes for the future. When someone loses their "other half" to death, their present and future are completely disrupted. They feel incomplete, lost, and shortchanged. There are also practical matters to consider, such as learning how to live and survive alone, worrying about finances and living arrangements, being a single parent to distressed children, and losing shared friends. Furthermore, the widow/widower must cope with all of these issues without their spouse—the person that they

---

19   M. Stroebe, W. Stroebe, and H. Schut, "Gender differences in adjustment to bereavement: An empirical and theoretical review," *Review of General Psychology*, 5 (2001): 62–83.

20   C. M. Sanders, *Grief: The Mourning After: Dealing with Adult Bereavement* (Oxford, England: Wiley, 1989).

previously relied on most for support. Given this, it is not surprising that conjugal bereavement is associated with an increased risk of depression, anxiety, and even death in the months immediately following the loss of a spouse.[21] Nevertheless, research finds that the majority of people who lose a spouse from natural causes tend to recover more quickly than expected.[22] Although they miss their spouse, most return to somewhat normal functioning, even six months after their loss.

While most of us expect to lose a parent at some point in the future, few of us are ready for the intense pain and grieving that follows it. Our parents symbolize our foundation, the pillar of our upbringing. Parents provide unconditional acceptance and love, for which there is no substitute, no matter what our age. As adults, the loss of our parents represents the severance of our role as someone's child, shifting one to the older generation or head of the family. While it is painful to lose a parent in adulthood, this is an expected transition that one can accept with time and understanding.

As a child or teen, however, the loss of a parent is one of the most immediately traumatizing events possible.[23] At a young age, children who experience the loss of a parent have to reconsider their assumptions of the world as a predictable, safe place. As children grow older, they continually reinterpret the death of a parent with their heightened development. While this often leads to greater acceptance and understanding, this continual reevaluation can mean that developmental transitions are more painful and intense for children who have experienced the loss of a parent.

The process of dealing with the death of a parent during childhood is often aggravated by additional changes, such as family restructuring, new expectations of children's behavior, the surviving parent's grief,

21   C. L. Hart, D. J. Hole, D. A. Lawlor, G. D. Smith, and T. F. Lever, "Effect of conjugal bereavement on mortality of the bereaved spouse in participants of the Renfrew/Paisley Study," *Journal of Epidemiology & Community Health*, 61(5) (2007): 455–460.

22   G. A. Bonanno, "Loss, trauma, and human resilience: Have we underestimated the human capacity to thrive after extremely aversive events?" *American Psychologist*, 59(1) (2004): 20.

23   J. Ribbens McCarthy, *Young People's Experiences of Loss and Bereavement: Towards an Interdisciplinary Approach* (McGraw-Hill Education [UK], 2006).

and death reminders—especially during occasions at which parents are usually present, such as school plays, holidays, and life cycle events.[24] Findings of studies suggest that the experience of parental death in childhood or adolescence is associated with a greater likelihood of mental and physical problems later in adulthood.[25] On the other hand, there is also evidence that parental death typically has smaller and less negative effects on children than parental divorce, particularly in the long-term.[26] This may be because the surviving parent tends to immortalize the deceased parent to their children, creating a feeling of connection, love, and support; whereas divorced parents may be more likely to show resentment and belittle ex-spouses, much to the confusion and discomfort of their children.[27]

Often overlooked, the loss of a sibling is especially traumatic and challenging. Siblings have a unique relationship—sharing a similar genetic background as well as their upbringing and personal history. Siblings are one of the most intimate relationships, often experiencing the best and worst moments together. The loss of a sibling represents the loss of a shared childhood, a missing piece in one's life, and a readjustment of one's place in the family. Nevertheless, the significance of the loss of a sibling is often underplayed. When one loses a sibling, friends and family may unknowingly focus on the welfare of the bereaved parent. For an adult who loses a sibling, the loss may entail additional responsibilities, such as helping their parents cope rather than focusing on

24   I. N Sandler, T. S. Ayers, S. A. Wolchik, J. Y. Tein, O. M. Kwok, R. A. Haine,...and J. L. Weyer, "The family bereavement program: efficacy evaluation of a theory-based prevention program for parentally bereaved children and adolescents," *Journal of Consulting and Clinical Psychology*, 71(3) (2003): 587.

25   N. A. Nicolson, "Childhood parental loss and cortisol levels in adult men," *Psychoneuroendocrinol* 29 (2004): 1012–18; K. J. Tsuchiya, E. Agerbo, P. B. Mortensen, "Parental death and bipolar disorder: A robust association was found in early maternal suicide," *J Affect Disord* 2005, 86 (2005): 151–59; L. J. Luecken, "Attachment and loss experiences during childhood are associated with adult hostility, depression, and social support," *J Psychosom Res*, 49 (2000): 85–91.

26   T. J. Biblarz and G. Gottainer, "Family structure and children's success: A comparison of widowed and divorced single-mother families," *Journal of Marriage and Family*, 62(2) (2000): 533–548.

27   Hetherington and Kelly, *For Better or For Worse*.

their own grief. For a young child who loses a sibling, the consequences are particularly severe. A young child not only has to cope with the confusion and pain of losing a sibling but also mourns the loss of their parents—whose tremendous grief may disrupt their ability to nurture their surviving children.

While grief is commonplace for bereaved individuals, there are a number of factors that have been shown to increase one's vulnerability following the loss of a loved one.[28]

- The length of time since the bereavement is one of the most important. People who are recently bereaved are at greater risk of problems compared with longer-term bereaved individuals. As the saying goes, time heals.
- The circumstances are also significant. When the loss is dramatic and sudden, it is associated with worse outcomes for the bereaved.
- The nature of the bereavement is critical. More generally, the loss of a child, including an adult child, is associated with more intense, prolonged grief than other types of bereavement.
- Multiple and concurrent losses further pose a more serious risk for the surviving loved ones.

Research points to a number of factors that help ease the pain of losing a loved one.

- A supportive social network has been shown to be significant for the recovery of bereaved individuals.[29]
- Friends and family lessen feelings of isolation and loneliness that follow the death of a loved one.
- For bereaved children, feeling safe and secure within a loving, supportive family is especially important.[30]

---

28   Sanders, *Grief: The Mourning After.*
29   W. Stroebe, H. Schut, and M. S. Stroebe, "Grief work, disclosure and counseling: do they help the bereaved?" *Clinical Psychological Review*; 25 (2005): 395–414.
30   K. K. Lin, I. N. Sandler, T. S. Ayers, S. A. Wolchik, and J. J. Luecken, "Resilience in Parentally Bereaved Children and Adolescents Seeking Preventive Services," *Journal of Clinical Child and Adolescent Psychology*, 33(4) (2004): 673–683.

- Religious beliefs and practices provide a context through which the bereaved can channel their loss.[31] Religious individuals have been shown to benefit from mourning rituals, which provide a sense of closure, connection with their community, and a set of beliefs that transcends death.[32]

In Jewish law, there are different stages of mourning that specify a framework to focus and express our grief, as well as provide guidance for family and friends. The Torah has established observances and rituals corresponding to a specific timetable through which the bereaved progress from greater to lesser phases of mourning. These stages assist mourners through the grieving process as they transition from utter despair and desolation to the normalcy of everyday existence. However, when we reach the final stages of mourning, our loved ones are not forgotten. They are continually memorialized through the recitation of special prayers, the lighting of memorial candles, and the giving of *tzedakah* (charity).

These practices serve to remind us that we are connected to our loved ones, even after their death. In Gan Eden, the soul continues to be involved in the lives of its descendants, interceding on our behalf in the Heavenly Court and guiding us to follow the right path. Since we are constricted by our physical bodies, however, we have limited awareness of their presence in our lives. In this world, we also intercede on behalf of our departed loved ones. The souls of our loved ones benefit from our positive deeds inspired in honor of their memory. Through the mitzvos we perform in their merit—including *tzedakah*, prayer, good deeds, and learning—we are able to help them attain an even greater level of elevation. In this way, a reciprocal relationship with our deceased loved ones continues to influence our present and future.

---

31   S. M. Clarke, B. J. Hayslip, R. Edmondson, C. A. Guarnaccia, "Religiosity, afterlife beliefs, and bereavement adjustment in adulthood," *Journal of Religious Gerontology*, 14 (2003): 207–24.

32   J. Davidson and K. J. Doka, eds., *Living with grief: At work, at school, at worship* (Psychology Press, 1999).

PHYSICAL AND MENTAL ILLNESS

I first had symptoms when I was seventeen. I woke up one morning and could not get out of bed. I could not feel my legs and could barely lift my head off the pillow. I went to the hospital and had every kind of test, but no one knew what was wrong with me. After everything was ruled out, I was diagnosed with chronic fatigue syndrome.

After university, I went to seminary for a year. I was unwell when I was in Israel and saw a neurologist there. They diagnosed me with multiple sclerosis (MS). I had mixed emotions. On one hand, I was utterly devastated to have this illness. It was a life sentence. On the other hand, I was so relieved to finally have someone who was taking me seriously, listening to me, and validating what I was saying and feeling after five years with no real answers.

I came back home with these test results and went to the hospital, where they redid all the tests. They said they could not give me a conclusive diagnosis, which meant that they couldn't give me any treatment. This was devastating. I had come to terms with the diagnosis and was feeling positive about the fact that there was a way forward. Suddenly, I was back to the beginning again.

So, I just carried on. I got married and went on with life. We had a baby. Although there were times when I was very weak, I always seemed to recover, but gradually, my health started to take a downward slide. I got pregnant again, so they wouldn't give me an MRI at that point. About a month after my baby was born, I finally received a diagnosis of MS. I was shocked because I was expecting them to tell me it was inconclusive again. I didn't know how to process that information, what I could do with it, and what it would mean for the future. I completely bottled up all the feelings I had about it. I felt numb.

I was advised to stop breastfeeding so I could begin treatment for the disease. Yet, the drugs I was given could only slow the progression of the disease, not stop it entirely. I still had sporadic relapses and there was no way of knowing when they would happen. The more relapses I had, the longer it took to recover and the more I was left with residual symptoms. In MS, the relapses are cumulative, so they lead to longer-term neurological damage.

I started to develop reactions to the medication, so they switched me onto a different drug. I was deteriorating at that point. I was walking with a splint and stick, and I had no stamina. My memory was non-existent and I found it hard to concentrate. I felt like I was failing in every area of my life and I didn't feel like a good mom.

I started going to a support group for MS. It was there that I first met someone who had had a hematopoietic stem cell transplant (HSCT). It was amazing to meet people I could identify with because before that I hadn't known anyone who could understand where I was coming from or what I was going through. Going to that group was a real turning point. I gained hope.

Then, I had a big relapse. This was the lowest point of my life. Right before, my husband and I had agreed to separate. I cannot put into words how desperate and isolated I felt. I couldn't get out of bed, and I didn't have anyone close by. I felt so alone. It hit me that I couldn't manage my life as a single mom. If I didn't do something drastic, the likelihood was that I would lose my independence, probably not too far down the line. At that point, I had nothing else to lose.

I decided to have the HSCT. The avenues I explored in the UK were not open to me, so I decided on Moscow. I started brainstorming ideas for fundraising. I set up a GoFundMe page and a Facebook page. In three months, we raised £60,000. It was amazing. It blew my mind. To feel that I was at such a low point, then all these people were telling me that I and my children matter. It was like climbing up a mountain and having people behind me, pushing me to go forward and cheering me on. I never could have done it if not for every single one of those people.

One of the biggest lessons I learned was that you have to tell people that you need help, however big or small. People will only know if you tell them. In asking someone, not only are you helping yourself, but you are helping them to bring good into the world, to do a mitzvah, and to share whatever gift or kindness they are able to contribute.

I believe that it is important to be open about the things that we are struggling with. People suffer on their own. There's a lot of stigma about having a disability. It took me a long time to be okay with myself and identify as a person that has a disability—because people look at you a bit differently. They see all the things you can't do rather than focusing on what you can. I've come to terms with the fact that there are things I can't do now in the way I used to. I have to adapt and find alternatives, and I'm okay with that. I am where I need to be. It's been a long journey to get to the point where I am

comfortable in my own skin, but I am. I'm proud of who I am, of what I have
achieved, and the example I have set for my children.

I truly believe that we all have challenges. Some of them we can see, and
some of them we cannot. Some of them we can understand the reason why,
and some of them we cannot. Hashem ultimately knows what's best for us,
and for whatever reason, we have to go through these experiences to get to
where we need to be. You have to trust that Hashem knows what is best for
you. My mantra has been: Focus on the things you can control and change,
and do the best you can with them. The things you cannot control, know that
Hashem can.

Statistics suggest that approximately one in three individuals live
with a chronic health problem, and one in two will experience a mental
health problem at some point in their lifetimes.[33] While a distinction
is often made between the mind and body, physical and mental health
are highly related. One-third of those with a long-term physical health
condition also have a mental health problem, and half of those with
a mental health problem have a long-term physical health condition.[34]
Physical health problems increase the risk of mental health problems
and vice versa. For example, studies have shown that those who have
mental health problems are at an increased risk of cardiovascular disease and cancer mortality.[35]

The co-occurrence of two or more diseases in an individual (i.e., comorbidity) is also high among mental disorders. There is high comorbidity between gambling, alcohol, drug addictions (which are classified
as mental health disorders), and other mental health disorders. A
mental health disorder in childhood or adolescence, such as untreated

---

33   Https://www.cdc.gov/media/releases/2011/a0901_adult_mental_Illness.html.
34   C. Naylor, M. Parsonage, D. McDaid, M. Knapp, M. Fossey, and A. Galea. *Long-Term*
     Conditions and Mental Health: The Cost of Comorbidities (The King's Fund and Centre for
     Mental Health, 2012).
35   H. Nabi, M. Kivimaki, R. De Vogli, M. G. Marmot, A. Singh-Manoux, "Positive and negative
     affect and risk of coronary heart disease: Whitehall II prospective cohort study," *BMJ*, 337
     (7660) (2008): 32–36; G. David Batty, Tom C. Russ, Emmanuel Stamatakis, Mika Kivimäki,
     "Psychological distress in relation to site specific cancer mortality: pooling of unpublished
     data from 16 prospective cohort studies," *BMJ*; 356 (2017): j108.

attention deficit hyperactivity disorder (ADHD), can also increase the risk of later disorders.[36] Self-harm and suicide are not considered mental health problems, but they are linked with mental illness, such as depression, anxiety, borderline personality disorder, and eating disorders.[37] Tragically, suicide is the second leading cause of death for fifteen to twenty-nine-year-olds globally.[38]

Most of the time, we cannot establish causality between co-occurring physical and mental illness, even if one preceded the other. There are some reasons, however, that may explain why they tend to co-occur:

- Those with mental health problems may engage in unhealthy behaviors such as smoking, overeating, and drug abuse as a form of self-medication.
- Those with chronic physical illness may experience financial struggles, lifestyle changes, and physical consequences of treatment, along with negative emotions such as fear and loneliness, which develop into mental health problems.
- Survivors of life-threatening physical illnesses, such as cancer, may experience adverse psychological symptoms, including post-traumatic stress disorder (PTSD), in the aftermath of recovery.[39]
- Physical and mental illness may be caused by overlapping environmental, behavioral, and genetic factors such as early exposure to trauma, recurrent stress, and a tendency toward risk-taking behavior.

---

36 Https://www.drugabuse.gov/sites/default/files/rrcomorbidity.pdf.

37 D. Nitkowski and F. Petermann, "Non-suicidal self-injury and comorbid mental disorders: a review," *Fortschr Neural Psychiatr*, 79 (1) (2011): 9–20; T. Paul, K. Schroeter, B. Dahme, and D. O. Nutzinger, "Self-Injurious Behavior in Women with Eating Disorders," *American Journal of Psychiatry*, 159 (3) (2002): 409–411.

38 "Preventing suicide," World Health Organization, file://Downloads/9789241564779_eng%20(1).pdf.

39 M. Y. Smith, W. H. Redd, C. Peyser, and D. Vogl, "Post-traumatic stress disorder in cancer: a review," *Psycho-Oncology: Journal of the Psychological, Social and Behavioral Dimensions of Cancer*, 8(6) (1999): 521–537; S. Swartzman, J. N. Booth, A. Munro, and F. Sani, "Posttraumatic stress disorder after cancer diagnosis in adults: A meta-analysis," *Depression and Anxiety*, 34(4) (2017): 327–339.

- Physical illness can also include symptoms of mental illness and vice versa. For example, symptoms of major depressive disorder can include fatigue, aches, cramps, and digestive problems.

Chronic physical and mental health problems exact a huge social and economic toll.[40] Along with the physical and mental burdens of the disease, those experiencing chronic physical and/or mental illness may be faced with discrimination and stigma, financial difficulties, and premature death. Living with physical and/or mental health problems often requires significant self and family management to cope with everyday life.[41] This might entail a regimen of hospital and therapeutic visits, multiple medications, self-monitoring, and significant life-style changes.

Mental and physical health problems further interfere with inter-personal relationships within the family as well as compromise family functioning. In spousal relationships, the divorce rate is higher in couples where mental health problems are present.[42] Findings suggest an elevated risk of divorce when the wife—but not the husband—has a physical illness.[43] For spouses, being a health caregiver can be marked by significant emotional pressure and isolation, and their own mental health needs are often overlooked.[44]

For parents, life changes dramatically with the diagnosis of a child's physical or mental health problem. Immediate changes in life routines are necessary, which have significant disruptive effects on the entire family. This is exacerbated by the difficulties encountered by parents in terms of their own coping, which may include feelings of devastation and uncertainty, conflicts in caregiving responsibilities in terms of other

40   Https://www.nami.org/.

41   M. Grey, K. Knafl, and R. McCorkle, "A framework for the study of self-and family manage-ment of chronic conditions," *Nursing Outlook*, 54(5) (2006): 278–286.

42   M. Idstad, F. A. Torvik, I. Borren, K. Rognmo, E. Røysamb, and K. Tambs, "Mental distress predicts divorce over 16 years: the HUNT study," *BMC Public Health* (2015): 15, 320.

43   A. Karraker and K. Latham, "In sickness and in health? Physical illness as a risk factor for marital dissolution in later life," *Journal of Health and Social Behavior*, 56(3) (2015): 420–435.

44   S. Lawn and J. McMahon, "The importance of relationship in understanding the experiences of spouse mental health carers," *Qualitative Health Research*, 24(2) (2014): 254–266.

children, financial strain, and concerns about the future.[45] However, there is great variability in parents' responses to a child's physical or mental health disability, depending on its severity and course. Research also highlights positive changes in their lives when parenting a child with a disability, such as personal growth, improved relationships with others, and increased spiritual values.[46]

For children, having parents with physical and/or mental health problems increases their risk of experiencing behavioral and emotional problems.[47] For children of parents with physical illness, this risk seems to be related to the number of daily hassles and the perception of stressfulness rather than by the severity of illness.[48] Furthermore, children whose parents have chronic disabilities often need to take on caregiving roles within their families. These young caregivers have been found to suffer from educational, physical, and mental problems but also show an increased sense of self-esteem, a close relationship with their parents, and early maturity.[49]

For children of parents with mental illness, their risk of poor outcomes is transmitted through their inherited genetic makeup, exposure to stress and anxiety in pregnancy, and poor parenting.[50] Children are often further exposed to economic disadvantage and marital conflict,

45   T. Heiman, "Parents of children with disabilities: Resilience, coping, and future expectations," *Journal of Developmental and Physical Disabilities*, 14(2) (2002): 159–171.

46   K. Scorgie and D. Sobsey, "Transformational outcomes associated with parenting children who have disabilities," *Mental Retardation*, 38(3) (2000): 195–206.

47   D. S. Sieh, A. M. Meijer, F. J. Oort, J. M. A. Visser-Meily, and D. A. V. Van der Leij, "Problem Behavior in children of chronically ill parents: a meta-analysis," *Clinical Child and Family Psychology Review*, 13(4) (2010): 384–397.

48   M. J. Dufour, A. M. Meijer, I. van de Port, and J. M. A. Visser-Meily, "Daily hassles and stress in the lives of children with chronically ill parents," *Nederlands Tijdschrift voor de Psychologie en haar Grensgebieden*, 61(2) (2006): 54–64; S. Verhaeghe, T. Defloor, and M. Grypdonck, "Stress and coping among families of patients with traumatic brain injury: A review of the literature," *Journal of Clinical Nursing*, 14(8) (2005): 1004–1012.

49   N. Chikhradze, C. Knecht, and S. Metzing, "Young carers: growing up with chronic illness in the family: A systematic review 2007–2017," *J of Compassionate Health Care* 4, 12 (2017).

50   J. Aldridge, "The experiences of children living with and caring for parents with mental illness," *Child Abuse Review: Journal of the British Association for the Study and Prevention of Child Abuse and Neglect*, 15(2) J. (2006): 79–88.

58   *Resilience*

both of which are associated with parental mental illness.[51] Much research has focused on the impact of the mother's depression on children: The risk of major depression is more than twice as high in children of depressed parents as in children of non-depressed parents.[52] For children and adolescents with depressed mothers, parenting likely plays a key role.[53] Depressed mothers show more hostility (negative emotions, criticism, negative facial expressions), fewer positive behaviors (pleasant emotions, praise, affectionate facial expressions), and more disengagement (ignoring, silence, gaze aversion) with their children than non-depressed mothers. Younger children, who are most dependent on their parents, experience the most impaired parenting associated with maternal depression. This may lead to insecure attachment and impaired social and problem-solving skills, which can cause further problems in childhood, adolescence, and later adult life.

Despite the high comorbidity between physical and mental illness, mental health is often neglected at the expense of a focus on physical health. People with physical health problems are often treated with urgency, while those with mental health problems are often left untreated or waiting for treatment for months or more.

There is also a significant gap between the prevalence of mental health problems and funding for prevention and treatment. Yet, research estimates that mental illness is the largest single source of the global burden of disease, and mental illness is more common, long-lasting, and impactful than other health conditions.[54]

---

51   C. Hammen, "Risk and protective factors for children of depressed parents," in S. S. Luthar (Ed.), *Resilience and Vulnerability: Adaptation in the Context of Childhood Adversities* (Cambridge University Press, 2003), pp. 50–75.

52   Ibid.

53   M. C. Lovejoy, P. A. Graczyk, E. O'Hare, and G. Neuman, "Maternal depression and parenting behavior: A meta-analytic review," *Clinical Psychology Review*, 20(5) (2000): 561–592.

54   S. C. Davies, *Annual Report of the Chief Medical Officer 2013, Public Mental Health Priorities: Investing in the Evidence* (2014), available from: gov.uk; D. Vigo, G. Thornicroft, and R. Atun, "Estimating the true global burden of mental illness," *The Lancet Psychiatry*, 3(2) (2016): 171–178.

There is further evidence that the prevalence of mental illness is increasing, especially for children and adolescents.[55] Among teenagers, there has been an increase in hospital admissions due to self-harming, an increase in the rate of overdose deaths from opioid misuse, and a rise in suicide.[56] Social media use, greater school pressures, and cyber-bullying are thought to play a role in this increase in mental health problems for teens. In the Jewish community, mental health problems may result from intense feelings of judgment and scrutiny from peers and pressures to conform from parents and teachers. There is also speculation that those who go "off the *derech*" ("leave the path") are at increased risk of mental illness, due to the loss of their identity and community.[57]

Considering the widespread and often devastating nature of mental health problems, why is mental illness such a neglected problem?

- A strong stigma attached to mental illness. Those with mental health problems face a double-edged sword. On one side, they struggle with the symptoms of mental illness. On the other, they are challenged by the stereotypes and prejudices that result from misconceptions about mental illness. As a consequence of both, people with mental disorders are often deprived of having a good job, stable marriage, safe housing, affordable and high-quality health care, and social connections with family and friends.[58]

---

55 Https://www.cambridge.org/core/journals/psychological-medicine/article/mental-health-and-wellbeing-trends-among-children-and-young-people-in-the-uk-19952014-analysis-of-repeated-crosssectional-national-health-surveys/AB71DE760C0027EDC5F5CF 0AF507FD1B.

56 Https://jamanetwork.com/journals/jama/article-abstract/2735809; https://youngminds. org.uk/blog/worrying-rise-in-teen-suicides/; https://www.nuffieldtrust.org.uk/resource/ hospital-admissions-as-a-result-of-self-harm-in-children-and-young-people; https://www. hhs.gov/ash/oah/adolescent-development/substance-use/drugs/opioids/index.html# prevalence.

57 Https://jewishweek.timesofisrael.com/once-shrouded-in-silence-now-young-jews-are-demanding-openness-about-mental-health-disorders/.

58 P. W. Corrigan. and A. C. Watson, "Understanding the impact of stigma on people with mental illness," *World Psychiatry*, 1(1) (2002): 16.

- A focus on reactive solutions to health. It is much easier to pre-scribe a medication than to address the myriad of factors that often accompany mental illness.
- An "either-or" attitude that either the disease is biological and no one is to blame *or* it is psychological and caused by patients, their parents, or their spouses.[59] This is short-sighted, as phys-ical and mental health constitute biological and environmental components, *both* of which need to be addressed for treatment.
- Diagnosis and treatment of mental health problems are not straightforward, especially given the overlapping symptomology among mental health disorders.
- A focus on short-term solutions rather than longer-term mental health promotion and prevention. While there has been much improvement in recent years, more is still needed to educate the public about mental health.

There are allusions to mental health problems in Jewish texts. One example provides instructions on how to deal with anxiety. A state-ment in *Mishlei* reads: *"Daagah b'lev ish yashchenah, v'davar tov yesam-chenah*—Anxiety in the heart of a person causes dejection, but a good word will turn it into joy."[60] The Hebrew word for dejection, *yashchenah*, has three different meanings, which may refer to three stages of heal-ing, including to suppress, to ignore, and to articulate:[61]

- Suppress the anxiety so that it does not overcome us.
- Disassociate from the source of the anxiety so it does not define who we are and can be replaced with something positive.
- Speak to someone about our anxiety who can provide us with guidance. In *Pirkei Avos* (Ethics of Our Fathers), we read, "Make for yourself a teacher" and "Get yourself a friend." This implies that we need to have people in our lives whom we respect, who

---

59 L. Eisenberg, "The social construction of the human brain," *American Journal of Psychiatry*, 152 (1995): 1563–1575.

60 *Mishlei* 12:25.

61 See https://www.chabad.org/theJewishWoman/article_cdo/aid/514028/jewish/A-Torah-Approach-to-Anxiety-Relief.htm.

understand and support us, and whom we can ask for guidance and advice, whether this is a friend, counselor, or therapist.[62]

Jews are not immune to the societal stigma attached to mental illness, which may lead to a reluctance in seeking professional help when facing mental health problems. There may be other reasons, such as concerns about potential marriage prospects through matchmaking or *shidduchim*. Whatever the reason(s), restricted access to professional services creates mental health inequalities in the Jewish community, furthering negative outcomes and leading to possible estrangement. Many symptoms of mental illness are treatable with talking and cognitive-behavioral therapies, complementary and alternative therapies like yoga and meditation, therapeutic communities, and medication. Diagnosis and appropriate treatment can make a world of difference to someone suffering from mental health problems.

More recently, there is a growing awareness of mental health problems, which is reaching the Jewish community. There is advocacy for the destigmatization of mental illness and improved access to mental health services. Online forums and support groups are becoming more common, fueled by young people's comfort with social media use. Many others are speaking out about their struggles with their own mental health problems and those of their family members who lost their lives to suicide and drug overdose. These individuals and organizations aim to reduce the stigma of mental illness and support those who are suffering through greater awareness and education. Their stories of struggle and triumph help others, especially those who have similar problems, to understand that they are not alone. As a community, we have come so far, but we still have a far way to go. Our Sages tell us: "If I am not for me, who is for me; and if I am [only] for myself, what am I? And if not now, when?"[63] This reminds us that each of us was created for a special purpose, and we are all obligated to make a difference to the world. There is no time like the present to ensure that no one suffers in silence.

---

62   Ibid.
63   *Pirkei Avos* 1:14.

CHILD MALTREATMENT

When I was around twelve, my mother remarried, and my stepdad was extremely difficult. I was not used to that. He had a big temper and was very unbending in what he wanted to be done. He was fanatical. I think he had a mental disorder; he was very abusive and aggressive.

As I had a normal childhood before that, I knew that this was not normal behavior. I was very reluctant to accept his behavior. I argued against it and stood my ground. There was no rhyme or reason for why he would explode. He would throw things around, and I felt like I was walking on eggshells all of the time. It was the type of environment where my emotional intelligence was heightened as I waited for him to erupt. I was also living in fear, as his temper was very violent. It was an unsettling environment.

I tried to keep a low profile. I even lived outside of the house in the garage for a while, with no plumbing or heating, just to get out of the house. I lived there since I could not handle the constant ups and downs—which I was still exposed to, even in the garage.

At the same time, I was very active and a good student. I did not let his instability affect my daily life and friendships. On the outside, everything seemed normal. But every night, I was scared, full of hate and anger. I remember I used to spend every night planning to run away. That was the poisonous, awful environment I was living in—every day. I was quite helpless; there were times I was suicidal. I was so unhappy that I did not want to live anymore.

When I was seventeen, I was forced to finally leave home, as he beat me up. My friends saw that I had bruises, and I realized I had to go. That was even scarier, as I didn't know what I was going to be doing or where I was going.

My friend and her dad came to pick me up. They took me to the police station, but I would not press charges. I couldn't do that to my mom. After we went to the police station, I wanted to get my things, and the policeman said, "I'll come with you." I didn't think this was necessary, but the policeman said that often in these situations they accuse you of stealing, and he wanted to be there as a witness, just in case. So, I put all my stuff in rubbish bags, including my passport, birth certificate, papers, everything. I knew I didn't want to come back. When I got to my friend's house, I thought I'd better phone my mom. The first thing she said to me is that I stole this and stole that. Nothing about whether I was okay or anything.

I had no home. I had no money, and my parents didn't care. The next day, my stepfather even called my school and told them them horrific lies about me.

I lived for a few months on friends' couches, moving from place to place. I had no idea where I was sleeping from day to day. As a kid, you just go with it. I finally got into a halfway house that supported me and got me on my feet. Without that, I'd be dead.

I had a lot of rejection from my parents, and it has stayed with me my whole life. I am still dealing with it to this day. The reason I push myself so hard is because I need the approval of other people. For a child to have had that rejection from their parents affects them on all levels. It affects your relationship with your spouse, to be able to show affection and communicate feelings. It is only through therapy that I can even speak about this today. When you are a child and you experience that level of rejection, it is the worst feeling in the world. So, you build a wall to avoid being rejected again. I have forgiven my parents, but I never forget. The rejection has made me who I am today, for good and for bad.

I was against marriage. My mother married this abusive man, and my father had been unfaithful. But, at the back of my mind, because I had been through an unstable upbringing, I knew I needed someone from a stable background, as I had no point of reference. I knew I needed someone to pull me up. When I found my spouse, he met every one of my requirements. When we got engaged, I was one hundred percent sure he was the one. He had the qualities I needed. I don't know how I knew that then, but I had this sixth sense that I needed someone like him. We have now been together for twenty-five years. He has helped me become who I am today, and I am very proud of what I have achieved in life.

I just celebrated my son's bar mitzvah and it was a very emotional time for me. You see pictures of your family, and you are in the room full of people, and you think, "This is the life I have created." If someone would have shown me this picture when I was sixteen and suicidal, I would not have believed it.

What I would tell others is that when you are in a period of intense abuse and trauma, which I was in for many years, know that "it, too, will pass." There is a light. It might even get worse before it gets better. Sometimes *when you are in an abusive relationship, you feel so hopeless, you want to die, but there are things you can do. There will come a point when you cannot carry on anymore. You have to act. At that point, it feels like the scariest time of your life because when you are in an abusive relationship, at least you know what to expect—but when you make that change, everything is unknown. But there is good in that. I think that is what got me through. I felt much safer than ever before. Even if you don't have anything, you don't have that fear of being abused. This has helped me throughout my life. I have been through a lot of difficult circumstances, but I have stuck it out. You know that however bad things get, there will be a tomorrow. There will be a time when you look back and this will just be a memory. You have to initiate the change, but if you do, you will get through it.*

Child maltreatment is the abuse and neglect of children under eighteen years of age. According to the World Health Organization, child maltreatment includes "all types of physical and/or emotional ill-treatment, sexual abuse, neglect, negligence, and commercial or other exploitation, which results in actual or potential harm to the child's health, survival, development, or dignity in the context of a relationship of responsibility, trust, or power." In terms of defining different types of abuse, childhood physical abuse is the intentional use of physical force, including shoving, hitting, suffocating, slapping, shaking, biting, throwing, punching, burning, or kicking, which results in harm or a high likelihood of harm to the child. Researchers note that most cases of child physical abuse start off as an extension of corporal punishment by parents.[64] Child sexual abuse is defined as the child subject to any behavior of sexual intent or content from an adult or older child. Childhood emotional abuse refers to verbal and non-verbal comments that are degrading, terrorizing, exploiting, corrupting, ignoring, isolating, hostile, or rejecting.[65] It is often difficult to distinguish this

---

64   A. Kadhusin and J. Martin, *Child Abuse: An Interactional Event* (New York: Columbia University Press, 1981).

65   S. N. Hart, R. B. Germain, and M. R. Brassard, eds., *Proceedings Summary of the International Conference on Psychological Abuse of Children and Youth* (Indiana University: Office for the Study of the Psychological Rights of the Child, 1983).

type of abuse from poor parenting, but it involves persistent acts of non-physical abuse that are harmful to the child.[66] Neglect involves the caregiver's failure to provide for the child's basic needs, despite their ability to do so. More recently, a child's exposure to domestic violence, which is also referred to as intimate partner violence, has also been included as a form of child maltreatment, as these types of violence often occur in the same household.[67]

Child maltreatment is a global problem with wide-ranging and long-lasting effects, which can span generations.[68] There is a strong link between child maltreatment and physical and mental health problems. While some physical problems resulting from childhood maltreatment can be detected immediately, such as head trauma, others can take years to surface. There is an association between childhood maltreatment and long-term health problems in adulthood, such as diabetes, cancer, stroke, and cardiovascular disease.[69]

Maltreatment causes children to feel a sense of mistrust, isolation, and fear, which can lead to psychological problems, such as mental illness, educational difficulties, and trouble forming positive relationships with friends and romantic partners.[70] Those who are maltreated often strive to be perfect as a way of preventing future maltreatment, coping with a sense of worthlessness, and providing some illusion of control.[71] This

---

66   Ibid.
67   T. Abramsky, C. H. Watts, C. Garcia-Moreno, et al, "What factors are associated with recent intimate partner violence? Findings from the WHO multi-country study on women's health and domestic violence," *BMC Public Health*, 11 (2011): 109–125; J. Osofsky, "Prevalence of children's exposure to domestic violence and child maltreatment: Implications for prevention and intervention," *Clinical Child and Family Psychology Review*, vol. 6, no. 3 (2003).
68   Https://www.childwelfare.gov/pubpdfs/long_term_consequences.pdf.
69   T. O. Afifi, H. L. MacMillan, M. Boyle, K. Cheung, T. Taillieu, S. Turner, and J. Sareen, "Child abuse and physical health in adulthood," *Health Reports*, 27 (2016): 10–18.
70   C. Doyle and D. Cicchetti, "From the cradle to the grave: The effect of adverse caregiving environments on attachment and relationships throughout the lifespan," *Clinical Psychology: Science and Practice*, 24(2) (2017): 203–217.
71   G. L. Flett and P. L. Hewitt, "Perfectionism and stress processes in psychopathology," in G. L. Flett and P. L. Hewitt, eds., *Perfectionism: Theory, Research, and Treatment* (American Psychological Association, 2002), 255–284.

perfectionism has been linked to further mental health problems, such as eating disorders, depression, and anxiety, as well as suicide.[72]

There is also evidence that childhood maltreatment may alter gene function without altering the DNA sequence (called epigenetics), explaining the enduring vulnerability to poor outcomes when in adulthood. In studies comparing the DNA of maltreated and non-maltreated children, findings indicate that maltreated children show numerous markers of diseases and alterations in stress-response related genes compared to non-maltreated children.[73]

Studies further suggest that maltreatment is associated with alteration in a range of neurocognitive systems, so maltreated children's internal processes (such as their emotions and thoughts) and how they perceive the external world often differ compared to non-maltreated children.[74] Maltreated children, for instance, may be hypervigilant to threatening situations and have a lower threshold for frustration and aggression.[75] Such hyperresponsiveness in perceiving and responding to potentially dangerous situations may be adaptive when living in a chaotic or violent home, but it can potentially lead to troublesome behavior and mental health problems later on.

Childhood maltreatment has further been linked with a heightened risk of engaging in antisocial behaviors. Maltreated children have a higher likelihood of engaging in criminal and violent activities,[76] and

72   G. L., Flett and P. L Hewitt, "A proposed framework for preventing perfectionism and promoting resilience and mental health among vulnerable children and adolescents," *Psychology in the Schools*, 51(9) (2014): 899–912.

73   A. A. Bouvette-Turcot, M. J. Meaney, and K. J. O'Donnell, "Epigenetics and Early Life Adversity: Current Evidence and Considerations for Epigenetic Studies in the Context of Child Maltreatment," in *The Biology of Early Life Stress* (Springer, Cham, 2018), 89–119.

74   E. J. McCrory, M. I. Gerin, and E. Viding, "Annual research review: childhood maltreatment, latent vulnerability and the shift to preventative psychiatry–the contribution of functional brain imaging," *Journal of Child Psychology and Psychiatry*, 58(4) (2017): 338–357.

75   E. J. McCrory, "Investigating the neurocognitive mechanisms that influence how mental health risk can unfold following maltreatment," *Biological Psychiatry: Cognitive Neuroscience and Neuroimaging*, 3(7) (2018): 579–580.

76   T. I. Herrenkohl, H. Jung, J. O. Lee, and M. H. Kim, "Effects of child maltreatment, cumulative victimization experiences, and proximal life stress on adult crime and antisocial behavior" (2017). Retrieved from https://www.ncjrs.gov/pdffiles1/nij/grants/250506.pdf.

they are more likely to have substance use disorder in adulthood than those who were non-maltreated.[77] Although most maltreated children do not go on to abuse or neglect their own children, they are more likely to do so compared to those who were not maltreated.[78] This creates an intergenerational cycle of maltreatment, where adults' parenting is influenced by their own childhood experiences of abusive and neglectful parenting.[79]

The prevalence of child maltreatment is difficult to estimate due to variations in its definition and the coverage and quality of official statistics.[80] Nevertheless, statistics suggest that maltreatment and violence frequently occur among family members, and children are exposed to much of this violence.[81] International studies, for example, estimate that a quarter of all adults report having been physically abused as children and one in five women and one in thirteen men report having been sexually abused as a child.[82] In the US, the prevalence of confirmed child maltreatment from 2004 to 2011 (as substantiated from Child Protection Services) indicate that one in eight children are victims by age eighteen, with the risk of maltreatment highest in the first year of life.[83]

77   N. G. Choi, D. M. DiNitto, C. N. Marti, and B. Y. Choi, "Association of adverse childhood experiences with lifetime mental and substance use disorders among men and women aged 50+ years," *International Psychogeriatrics*, 29 (2017): 359–372.

78   M. Yang, S. A. Font, M. Ketchum, and Y. K. Kim, "Intergenerational transmission of child abuse and neglect: Effects of maltreatment type and depressive symptoms," *Children and Youth Services Review*, 91 (2018): 364–371.

79   Child Welfare Information Gateway (2018), "Cycle of abuse." Retrieved from https://www.childwelfare.gov/topics/can/impact/long-term-consequences-of-child-abuse-and-neglect/abuse/.

80   World Health Organization, https://www.who.int/news-room/fact-sheets/detail/child-maltreatment.

81   J. Osofsky, "Prevalence of children's exposure to domestic violence and child maltreatment: Implications for prevention and intervention," *Clinical Child and Family Psychology Review*, vol. 6, no. 3 (2003).

82   Ibid.

83   C. Wildeman, N. Emanuel, J. M. Leventhal, E.Putnam-Hornstein, J.Waldfogel, and H. Lee, "The prevalence of confirmed maltreatment among US children, 2004 to 2011," *JAMA pediatrics*, 168(8) (2014): 706–713.

A study of 372 diversely religious adult Jews in the United States found that prevalence of sexual abuse in childhood was equivalent to national rates. All religious groups reported similar levels of sexual abuse, although there was a greater prevalence of childhood sexual abuse among formerly Orthodox individuals (those who were raised as Orthodox but are no longer observant).[84]

In Israel, a study conducted from 2011 to 2013, using firsthand accounts from Jewish children (8,239) aged twelve (sixth grade), fourteen (eighth grade), and sixteen (tenth grade) found that one-half of the Jewish children reported being physically, emotionally, or sexually abused.[85]

- 29.1% of Jewish children reported emotional abuse, 17.7% reported sexual abuse, 16% reported emotional neglect, 14.6% reported physical neglect, 14.7% reported physical abuse, and 8.6% reported that they had been exposed to violence within the family.
- These rates are comparable with a lifetime prevalence of child maltreatment in North America, which show that 23.9% had emotional abuse, 18.2% sexual abuse, 30.1% physical and emotional neglect, and 18.1% physical abuse (based on a study which averaged rates across multiple studies).[86]
- Jewish boys were more likely to experience physical abuse and neglect than girls, and Jewish girls were more likely to be exposed to domestic violence than boys.
- The likelihood of exposure increased with age. Jewish children reported a 13.2% rate of sexual abuse at age twelve, which increased to 23.9% at age sixteen. In 46.5% of the cases of sexual

84   D. H. Rosmarin, S. Pirutinsky, M. Appel, T. Kaplan, and D. Pelcovitz, "Childhood sexual abuse, mental health, and religion across the Jewish communitym," *Child Abuse & Neglect*, 81(2018): 21–28.

85   R. Lev-Wiesel, Z. Eisikovits, M. First, R. Gottfried, and D. Mehlhausen, "Prevalence of child maltreatment in Israel: A national epidemiological study," *Journal of Child & Adolescent Trauma*, 11(2) (2018): 141–150.

86   Ibid.

abuse and 78.5% of the cases of physical abuse, the perpetrator was a family member.[87]

- Both Jewish boys (17.6%) and girls (17.7%) reported similar rates of sexual abuse in the Israeli study,[88] but other studies suggest that girls (20.4%, an average of 106 studies)[89] have a higher lifetime prevalence rate than boys (14.1%, an average of 56 studies).[90] The authors of the study suggest that one possible explanation for the higher prevalence of boys who have experienced sexual abuse in the Israeli study is the growing social legitimacy for males to disclose sexual abusive experiences.[91] Another possible explanation that the authors suggest is that boys within the religious educational school system are separated from girls and educated by male teachers, thereby possibly making them more vulnerable to violence from other males.[92]

The Torah has a non-equivocal stance about which relationships are forbidden and which are allowed.[93]

- According to the Torah, a man cannot marry specific close blood relatives, the ex-wives of specific close blood relatives, a woman who has not been properly divorced from her previous husband, the daughter or granddaughter of his ex-wife, or the sister of his ex-wife during the ex-wife's lifetime.

---

87 G. Moody, R. Cannings-John, K. Hood, A. Kemp, and M. Robling, "Establishing the international prevalence of self-reported child maltreatment: a systematic review by maltreatment type and gender," *BMC Public Health*, 18(1), (2018): 1164.

88 R. Lev-Wiesel, Z. Eisikovits, M. First, R. Gottfried, and D. Mehlhausen, "Prevalence of child maltreatment in Israel: A national epidemiological study, *Journal of Child & Adolescent Trauma*, 11(2) (2018): 141–150.

89 G. Moody, R. Cannings-John, K. Hood, A. Kemp, and M. Robling, "Establishing the international prevalence of self-reported child maltreatment: a systematic review by maltreatment type and gender," *BMC Public Health*, 18(1), (2018): 1164.

90 Ibid.

91 R. Lev-Wiesel, Z. Eisikovits, M. First, R. Gottfried, and D. Mehlhausen, "Prevalence of child maltreatment in Israel: A national epidemiological study, *Journal of Child & Adolescent Trauma*, 11(2) (2018): 141–150.

92 Ibid.

93 https://www.chabad.org/library/article_cdo/aid/290031/jewish/Human-or-Beast.htm.

- The Torah is also extremely vigilant about all contact and inter-action between the sexes, which helps to prevent any inappropriate behavior. Numerous laws forbid a man and woman who are not married to each other from being alone together, which also applies to an adult and child unless they are a parent with their own child.
- The Torah completely forbids any physical contact between an unmarried man and a woman, a man (who is not the father) and a girl, or a woman (who is not the mother) and a boy.

There are also Torah prohibitions against physical violence.[94] In Rabbinic literature, there are passages where parents are warned of the negative effects of physical and emotional abuse.[95] For example: Rav Chisda said, "A man should never impose excessive fear upon his household, or else he may be the cause of great tragedy."[96]

Similarly, the Torah commands us to be careful with our words: "You shall reprove your neighbor, but incur no guilt because of him."[97] Thus, we are taught that rebuke should only emanate from love and not hurt someone in the process. The Chafetz Chaim wrote about the concept of *shemiras ha'lashon*, guarding one's tongue. There are ten types of negative speech, including *onaas devarim*. The Torah prohibits *onaas devarim*, which are words that cause a person needless pain, including all forms of insult. The pain of verbal maltreatment should not be understated. As the Vilna Gaon said, "Speaking hurtfully to someone is worse than hitting them. When you hit someone, you affect his body. Words go much deeper. Moreover, bruises eventually heal. But the negative effect of words may never be healed."[98]

Childhood maltreatment involves a significant deviation from the normal environment that is required to successfully raise a child. Sadly, research suggests that resilience is especially difficult for maltreated

---

94   https://www.chabad.org/library/article_cdo/aid/3488906/jewish/The-Prohibition-Against-Physical-Violence.htm.

95   Https://www.myjewishlearning.com/article/must-one-honor-an-abusive-parent/.

96   *Gittin* 6b.

97   *Vayikra* 19:17.

98   Zelig Pliskin, *Consulting the Wise* (Benei Yakov Publications: New York, 1991).

children.[99] One reason is that child maltreatment often goes hand in hand with other problems such as conflict between parents, having a parent with mental health problems or who uses drugs, and poverty.[100] Another reason is often the lack of positive factors in maltreated children's lives. For example, a good relationship with parents is protective, but maltreated children, by definition, are unlikely to receive high-quality parenting.[101]

Nevertheless, maltreated children are not destined to experience lives of hardship. Evidence suggests that some children fare better than others.[102] This is likely due to the variability in maltreatment experiences. Children who are older when maltreatment occurs and those who are exposed to shorter, less severe experiences of abuse are more likely to be resilient compared to those who experienced more severe, prolonged abuse.[103]

Given the long-lasting and devastating consequences of child maltreatment, the most effective course is preventing this tragedy from happening in the first place. For this reason, it is important for parents to learn how to protect their children and teach them how to protect themselves. Here are some suggestions.[104]

- Within the family, teach children about personal safety in an age-appropriate way from age three years, providing additional

99   D. Cicchetti and M. Lynch, "Failures in the expectable environment and their impact on individual development: The case of child maltreatment," in D. Cicchetti and D. J. Cohen, eds., *Wiley Series on Personality Processes: Developmental Psychopathology, Vol. 2: Risk, Disorder, and Adaptation* (John Wiley & Sons, 1995), 32–71.

100   M. Lynch and D. Cicchetti, "An ecological-transactional analysis of children and contexts: The longitudinal interplay among child maltreatment, community violence, and children's symptomatology," *Development and Psychopathology*, 10(2) (1998): 235–257.

101   K. E. Bolger and C. J. Patterson, "Sequelae of child maltreatment: Vulnerability and resilience," *Resilience and Vulnerability: Adaptation in the Context of Childhood Adversities* (2003): 156–181.

102   J. B. Klika and T. I. Herrenkohl, "A review of developmental research on resilience in maltreated children," *Trauma, Violence, & Abuse*, 14(3) (2013): 222–234.

103   K. E. Bolger and C. J. Patterson, "Sequelae of child maltreatment: Vulnerability and resilience," *Resilience and Vulnerability: Adaptation in the Context of Childhood Adversities* (2003): 156–181.

104   Https://www.chabad.org/library/article_cdo/aid/1707466/jewish/Things-You-Need-to-Know-About-Child-Molesters.htm.

information as children mature. Role-playing is an effective and proactive way for children to learn how to protect themselves.

- Be aware of the characteristics of perpetrators. They are usually charming, friendly, and extremely manipulative. They groom children from an early age, gaining their trust and friendship over time. While all children are at risk, perpetrators most often seek out shy and naive children, those with disabilities, and those who are troubled, experiencing loneliness or emotional neglect.
- Be wary and communicate calmly if a child seems uncomfortable or negative about, receives gifts and special favors from, and/or meets privately in a room with an adult or older teen.
- If you suspect abuse, do not blame the child and do not attempt to confront the perpetrator; call the police immediately.
- If child maltreatment occurs, trauma-informed care is critical to limit its long-term consequences. In trauma-informed care, professionals acknowledge a child's history of trauma, provide appropriate care to alleviate its effects, and prevent future maltreatment.[105]

---

105   Https://www.cdc.gov/violenceprevention/childabuseandneglect/prevention.html.

Chapter Four

WHAT FOSTERS RESILIENCE?

We are all capable of astonishing resistance, adaptation, recovery, and resilience in the face of adversity. When faced with a major setback, what enables our resilience? Psychological research has identified three sets of positive factors that strengthen us during challenging times. These are referred to as protective factors, as they protect us from experiencing negative outcomes during stressful circumstances.[1]

- **Personal strengths,** such as having positive beliefs about ourselves, actively coping with problems, and believing in a higher purpose
- **Family strengths,** including nurturing relationships, engaging in healthy communication, having an organized and structured family life, and creating a meaningful family system

1   N. Garmezy, "Reflections and commentary on risk, resilience, and development," *Stress, Risk, and Resilience in Children and Adolescents: Processes, Mechanisms, and Interventions,* (1996):1–18; A. Masten and A. Barnes, "Resilience in children: developmental perspectives," *Children,* 5(7) (2018): 98.

- **Support systems,** such as having positive friendships, being part of a supportive community, and spending time in nature

These are not remarkable qualities; rather, they are commonplace characteristics and experiences that are evident in most people and families. Fostering resilience is fundamentally human. It involves cultivating an understanding of ourselves and building a connection with others and the wider world.

Nor are these factors show-stopping, one-time displays of greatness. Rather, they are incremental and continuous practices that we engage in on a daily basis, which compound and build over time. Singular or intermittent experiences will not uphold our capacity for resilience. Our interactions with others, as well as how we regard ourselves, must be continually reinforced and renewed.

> What fosters resilience are not extraordinary but commonplace characteristics and experiences that are evident in most people and families.

The importance of these factors differs across individuals as well as situations.[2] What is most important for a child may be different from what is most important for an adult. For young children, having an early secure attachment to their parents is a key process that influences their adjustment and relationships with others. For adults, personal strengths such as active coping are more salient, especially when there are others depending on us.

Resilience also requires different strengths depending on the particular challenge at hand. When facing a trauma that is uncontrollable, unforeseen, and unalterable, finding meaning and maintaining faith are especially important. When facing a shorter-term and more manageable situation, problem-solving may be more relevant. What is important to highlight is that there are many different pathways to resilience. In other words, there is no single magic formula. It is the

---

2   A. J. Sameroff and L. M. Gutman, "Contributions of risk research to the design of successful interventions," *Intervention with Children and Adolescents: An Interdisciplinary Perspective* (New York: Pearson Education, 2004), 9–26.

presence of these factors, rather than their specificity, that seems to be the common denominator for positive adjustment following adversity.

The protective factors examined in this book are not an exhaustive list. Those that are covered, however, are what many consider to be the most significant for resilience. For the most part, these are the most commonly observed in different cultures, although there are variations in how they are enacted, for example, in terms of how people interpret, understand, and make sense of life events; the ways that families interact with one another and socialize their children; the salience of rituals and routines; and the extent to which support systems are available to provide care and consolation.[3]

STRENGTHS EXERCISE

An understanding of your own character strengths (our positive traits that influence how we think, feel, and act) is beneficial for fostering resilience. Positive psychology has identified twenty-four character strengths, which can be measured using the Values in Action (VIA) survey.[4] These character strengths are related to one of the following six broader virtues: (1) wisdom and knowledge, (2) courage, (3) humanity, (4) justice, (5) temperance, and (6) transcendence.[5]

Wisdom and knowledge help you to gather and use knowledge.

1. Perspective
2. Creativity
3. Curiosity
4. Open-mindedness
5. Love of learning

3   M. Ungar, "Resilience, trauma, context, and culture," *Trauma, Violence, and Abuse*, 14(3) (2013): 255–266.

4   C., Peterson and M. E. Seligman, *Character Strengths and Virtues: A Handbook and Classification*, Vol. 1 (Oxford University Press, 2004).

5   See https://www.viacharacter.org/character-strengths for a description of these strengths and how you might apply them.

Courage helps you to exercise your free will and face adversity.

   6. Zest
   7. Bravery
   8. Integrity
   9. Persistence

Humanity helps you to have positive interpersonal relationships.

  10. Love
  11. Kindness
  12. Social intelligence

Justice helps you to connect to the community or in group-based situations.

  13. Teamwork
  14. Fairness
  15. Leadership

Temperance helps you manage habits and protect against excess.

  16. Prudence
  17. Forgiveness
  18. Modesty
  19. Self-regulation

Transcendence helps you to connect to the larger universe and provide meaning.

  20. Humor
  21. Appreciation of Beauty
  22. Gratitude
  23. Hope
  24. Spirituality

We each possess these twenty-four character strengths in different degrees, which give each of us a distinctive character strengths profile. We are truly one of a kind. "The number of potential character strengths profiles is exponentially greater than the number of people living on our planet."⁶ You can discover your character strengths profile by taking the scientifically validated VIA Survey, available at: https://www.viacharacter.org/survey/account/register.

Your profile can help you have a better understanding of your greatest strengths, referred to as your "signature strengths." With this knowledge, you can consider how to utilize your signature strengths in everyday life. For example, let's say that one of your signature strengths is teamwork. This means that you thrive in a team, such as a work group or a sports team, but this can also refer to your family, marriage, or community. A person whose signature strength is teamwork is a dedicated, reliable, and contributing member to a small group or team of people who share the same goals. You can use this strength by

- focusing on creating a sense of cohesion and connection among your loved ones;
- energizing work colleagues to accomplish their goals;
- encouraging family brainstorming to solve problems;
- leading community-building projects.

An understanding of your lesser strengths can also help you to enhance them. For example, let's say that one of your lesser strengths is curiosity. Curiosity involves considering novel and productive ways to conceptualize, explore, and discover new things. Those who are curious are open to novel experiences and have a natural desire to learn. Curiosity is one of the five strengths that has been shown most strongly to relate to life satisfaction, along with love, hope, gratitude, and zest.⁷ You can encourage this strength by

- paying closer attention to your environment and those around you;
- focusing on those aspects of life that you usually ignore or take for granted;

6   Https://www.viacharacter.org/character-strengths.
7   N. Park, C. Peterson, and M. E. Seligman, "Strengths of character and well-being," *Journal of Social and Clinical Psychology*, 23(5) (2004): 603–619.

- asking "why" and "how" questions more often to your co-workers, family members, and friends;
- finding novel reasons for engaging in activities that you usually find tiresome and boring.

Understanding your character strengths can be an important part of building resilience.[8] Research has shown that when someone learns their own strengths and applies them in novel ways, this can improve their well-being.[9] Many of the exercises in this book foster resilience through improving one's character strengths (such as perseverance, self-regulation, judgment, perspective, hope, and gratitude). Character strengths also work hand in hand when strengthening our families, friendships, and communities (such as love, teamwork, and leadership). You may wish to see the see the VIA website for further ideas on how to apply your character strengths in different situations.[10]

After you have completed the survey and obtained your results, list your top five signature strengths. Answer the following questions, considering each of your signature strengths, in turn.

- How does this strength influence your day-to-day life?
- How do you feel when using this strength?
- How does this strength influence your energy levels and motivation?
- Can you think of new ways to use and build this strength?
- How has this strength helped you deal with difficult situations in the past?
- How can this strength help you in the future?

---

8   M. L. Martínez-Martí and W. Ruch, "Character strengths predict resilience over and above positive affect, self-efficacy, optimism, social support, self-esteem, and life satisfaction," *The Journal of Positive Psychology*, 12(2) (2017): 110–119.

9   M. E. Seligman, T. A. Steen, N. Park, and C. Peterson, "Positive psychology progress: empirical validation of interventions," *American Psychologist*, 60(5) (2005): 410–421.

10   Https://www.viacharacter.org/character-strengths.

PERSONAL STRENGTHS

When we consider someone who is resilient, we might imagine historical and cinematic heroes, those strong and silent types who sacrifice their own needs and desires to achieve their primary goal. These individuals are not shown to waver; we do not see them consider different options, weighing which one is the right strategy for a particular situation. Rather, they are full of action; they are quick-thinking and quick-doing.

In psychological research, in contrast, the personal qualities that transmit resilience are not reactive but proactive. They involve reflection, (re)consideration, and (re)evaluation. The way we view ourselves, how we respond to problems, and our relationship with God are all integral to our ability to bounce forward from life's mishaps. Resilience is cultivated when we

- guide our (often unconscious) feelings about ourselves and our environment in order to recognize and support our inner strengths and capabilities;
- process and manage our emotions, thoughts, and behaviors in response to stressful situations in ways that are growth orientated;
- actively work on improving our relationship with God.

Personal strengths that foster resilience can be placed into three main categories, which include:

- **Beliefs about ourselves**: Do you see yourself as capable? Do you expect good things to happen to you? Do you believe that you can grow and learn from failure? Do you feel compassion for yourself?
- **Self-regulation of our thoughts, emotions, and actions**: Do you know how to actively cope with problems? Can you reframe a challenging situation as something positive? Can you laugh, be happy, and feel gratitude, even during difficult times? Do you know how to be present and fully engaged in whatever you are doing at the moment?

- **Existential beliefs**: Do you have a strong faith and trust in God? Are you hopeful about the future? Do you believe that what happens to you has a purpose and is meaningful?

Beliefs about Ourselves

> "You are wherever your thoughts are. Make sure
> your thoughts are where you want to be."
>
> Rebbe Nachman of Breslov[11]

How we feel about ourselves is fundamental to our ability to handle adversity. One important self-belief, **self-efficacy**, is whether we believe in our ability to succeed in a particular situation. Albert Bandura, known as the father of self-efficacy, defined it as "people's beliefs about their capabilities to produce designated levels of performance that exercise their influence over events that affect their lives."[12] Self-efficacy influences whether we think, feel, and act in ways that are self-enhancing (rather than self-limiting). When we lack a strong sense of self-efficacy, we are more likely to be self-limiting, holding ourselves back from achieving what we are truly capable of.

When we feel efficacious, on the other hand, we are motivated to persist even when facing difficulties. Feeling efficacious encourages us to pursue challenging pathways (rather than taking the easy road).[13] When we believe that we have the capability to succeed, we try harder to do so and thus are more likely to achieve in our endeavors. However, when we feel we lack the capability, we are more likely to give up easily and experience a negative emotional response. As Bandura put it, "If

---

11   M. Mykoff, *Empty Chair: Finding Hope and Joy—Timeless Wisdom from a Hasidic Master Rebbe Nachman of Breslov* (Jewish Lights Publishing, 1994).

12   A. Bandura, "The explanatory and predictive scope of self-efficacy theory," *Journal of Social and Clinical Psychology*, 4(3) (1986): 359–373.

13   L. M. Gutman and I. Schoon, "The impact of non-cognitive skills on outcomes for young people," Education Endowment Foundation, 59(22.2) (2013): 2019.

self-efficacy is lacking, people tend to behave ineffectually, even though they know what to do."[14]

Whether or not we believe in ourselves is a product of our experiences at home, school, work, and the wider world. Our beliefs about what we can (or cannot!) accomplish come from our own experiences as well as what we are told from our parents, teachers, friends, and employers.

According to Bandura, there are four important sources of self-efficacy, and their interplay determines how we view our own capabilities.

- The most important source is our mastery experiences. When we succeed at something, this boosts our self-efficacy, and when we fail, we may doubt ourselves and have lowered self-confidence. If we experience only easy successes, we come to expect them and then become discouraged by failure. Self-efficacy is developed when we overcome obstacles and experience success through our own hard work.

- Another source of self-efficacy is through the vicarious experiences of social models. When we see people similar to us succeed through their sustained effort, this raises our beliefs that we too have the capabilities to master comparable activities. The opposite is also true: when other people like us fail despite their efforts, this reduces our own feelings of capability. The more strongly that we believe someone is similar to us, the more we will be influenced by their successes and failures.

- Social persuasion is the third influence. When we are told that we have the capabilities to master specific activities, then we are more likely to put in the necessary effort to succeed. On the other hand, when we are persuaded that we lack the capability, we tend to avoid challenging activities that cultivate potentialities, and we give up easily in the face of difficulties. Being told that we are efficacious, on its own, is rarely enough to boost self-efficacy. Once someone experiences failure, these boosts are not sustained. With this in mind, it is important to do more than simply give

---

14   A. Bandura, *Social Foundations of Thought and Action* (Englewood Cliffs, NJ, 1986).

verbal praise. Rather, in order to raise feelings of efficacy, it is necessary to structure situations that bring small successes and avoid situations, at least initially, that are likely to produce failure (as efficacy develops, one should be more persistent in the face of disappointment). Also, it is important to measure success in terms of self-improvement rather than through comparison to others.

- A final source of self-efficacy is how we feel both emotionally and physically. When we experience a stressful reaction to an event, we may see this as a sign of poor performance. How we are feeling more generally also affects how we judge our self-efficacy. When we are in a good mood, we are more likely to see ourselves as efficacious, and when we are in a bad mood, we are more likely to judge ourselves as lacking. What is important is not the intensity of our physical and emotional reactions, but how we perceive and interpret them. Those who have a high self-efficacy are more likely to view physical and emotional stress as normative and even energizing. Those who have a low self-efficacy, on the other hand, are more likely to view stress as debilitating and a sign of weakness.

Self-reflection and self-awareness are important parts of our self-efficacy. Self-efficacy can be nurtured when we reflect on our self-perceptions and try to understand how they influence our actions. When we are hesitant to try something new, we should question why this is so. Are we afraid of failure? Do we believe we lack the ability? Did we experience a traumatic situation in the past that is stopping us from attempting challenging activities? With such an awareness, we can challenge and push through self-limitations that are preventing our growth and achievement.

SELF-EFFICACY EXERCISE

"Is there something that you really want or wish would happen? Focus every ounce of your concentration on that thing or event. Visualize it in

fine detail. When your desire is strong enough and
your concentration intense enough, you can make
it come true."[15]

Rebbe Nachman of Breslov

Studies have shown that visualization can increase our self-efficacy.[16]
This visualization practice helps us to imagine our goals and how we
might achieve them.

1. Visualize three goals that you would like to achieve this year.
2. Write these goals down.
3. Visualize potential barriers you might experience.
4. Write these potential barriers down.
5. Visualize possible approaches that you could use to counter these
   barriers. Imagine yourself using these approaches successfully.
6. Write these approaches down.
7. Review and revise these as necessary.

Motivational self-talk is another strategy that has been shown to promote self-efficacy.[17] Self-talk (our inner voice that provides a running
dialogue throughout the waking day) reflects our beliefs in our own
capabilities. When we engage in motivational self-talk, we deliberately
change our internal conversations to boost self-confidence, reduce self-
limiting beliefs, and empower ourselves to put our best foot forward. To
practice motivational self-talk, follow these steps.

15 M. Mykoff, *Empty Chair: Finding Hope and Joy—Timeless Wisdom from a Hasidic Master, Rebbe Nachman of Breslov* (Jewish Lights Publishing, 1994).
16 L. Morin and G. Latham, "The effect of mental practice and goal setting as a transfer of training intervention on supervisors' self-efficacy and communication skills: An exploratory study," *Applied Psychology*, 49(3) (2000): 566–578; O. B. Davidson, D. B. Feldman, and M. Margalit, "A focused intervention for 1st-year college students: Promoting hope, sense of coherence, and self-efficacy," *The Journal of psychology*, 146(3) (2012): 333–352.
17 A. Hatzigeorgiadis, N. Zourbanos, C. Goltsios, and Y. Theodorakis, "Investigating the functions of self-talk: The effects of motivational self-talk on self -efficacy and performance in young tennis players," *The Sport Psychologist*, 22(4) (2008): 458–471; Y. K. Chang, L. A. Ho, F. J. H. Lu, C. C. Ou, T. F. Song, and D. L. Gill, "Self-talk and softball performance: The role of self-talk nature, motor task characteristics, and self-efficacy in novice softball players," *Psychology of Sport and Exercise*, 15(1) (2014): 139–145.

1. Set aside a couple of minutes to engage in motivational self-talk every day.
2. Stand in front of the mirror and say positive motivational statements that you need to hear. It is usually more effective to say these statements aloud rather than just thinking them.

   - Your statement can focus on praise, such as: "I did really well today. I spoke clearly and maintained eye contact, even though I felt nervous. I am really proud of myself."
   - You can also choose to focus on your past successes and/or the successes of role models who are similar to you such as: "My friend went to the event last year and really enjoyed it. That friend is also somewhat shy and reserved like me. I'll have a good time too."
   - You can counter negative emotions: "It is okay to feel apprehensive about the event tomorrow. That is totally normal. I will go and meet new people. I will be fine."
   - You can further dispute self-limiting beliefs: "I have a self-limiting belief that I am socially awkward. This belief is preventing me from going to new places and meeting new people. I might be a little shy, but I have several close friends who like spending time with me."
   - You can also offer practical solutions to boost self-efficacy, starting with smaller, achievable goals: "I am going to start introducing myself to one new person each week."

3. You may consider keeping a journal of your self-talk so you can track your progress.

Learned optimism is another important belief that promotes resilience when facing setbacks. Learned optimism is considered a learned habit of viewing ourselves and the world in a positive light.[18] It is the belief that good things will happen and challenges are temporary. This

---

18   M. E. Seligman, *Learned optimism: How to change your mind and your life* (New York: Vintage, 2006).

contrasts with learned helplessness, which is when someone faces a continuous negative circumstance and believes that nothing will make a difference in its resolution.[19] As a result, they stop trying to improve their situation, even when they have the ability to do so.[20] As we might expect, people who have optimistic beliefs have better health outcomes and experience less stress.[21] They also cope better with adversity and are more likely to make positive changes in response to problems than those with pessimistic beliefs.[22]

Whether we lean toward learned optimism or learned helplessness can be distinguished based on our explanatory beliefs concerning why events happen in our lives. Differences in explanatory styles can be classified according to the 3 Ps.[23]

- **Personalization** is when we believe that a situation happened because of internal factors. Those who are learned optimists view positive events as a result of internal reasons (such as their own efforts) and negative events as a result of external factors (such as bad luck). In contrast, those who are learned helpless view negative events due to internal causes (such as their own incompetence), which can lead to self-blame and self-criticism, and positive events due to external causes (such as being in the right place at the right time).
- **Permanence** is when we believe that a situation is permanent. Learned optimists view negative events as temporary—which allows them to accept the situation and adapt for the future—and positive events as permanent. Those who are learned helpless view positive events as temporary and negative events

---

19   C. Peterson, S. F. Maier, and M. E. P. Seligman, *Learned helplessness: a theory for the age of personal control* (Oxford University Press, 1993).

20   Ibid.

21   H. N. Rasmussen, M. F. Scheier, and J. B. Greenhouse, "Optimism and physical health: A meta-analytic review," *Annals of Behavioral Medicine*, 37(3) (2009): 239–256.

22   C. S. Carver, and J. Connor-Smith "Personality and coping," *Annual Review of Psychology*, 61(2010): 679–704.

23   M. E. Seligman, *Learned optimism: How to change your mind and your life* (New York: Vintage, 2006).

as permanent and unchangeable. As a result, they are less likely to initiate changes to improve a stressful circumstance.

- **Pervasiveness** is when we believe that a situation applies to all areas of our life. Learned optimists see negative events as applying to only one area of their life, which allows them to be positive about other aspects of their life. When good events happen, on the other hand, learned optimists see these as happening in other aspects of their life as well. Those who are learned helpless, in contrast, see setbacks as pervasive, which means that they believe they will fail in everything they attempt.

What is important to highlight is that the 3 Ps are learned thought processes; in other words, we can learn and "un-learn" them. According to Seligman, anyone can learn the techniques to become a more optimistic person.[24]

> Anyone can learn the techniques to become a more optimistic person.

LEARNING OPTIMISM EXERCISE

Here is an exercise that may help you to increase your optimism.[25] As with all of these exercises, this is an ongoing process that takes time and may need to be repeated as necessary.

1. Consider a difficult experience that is happening now.
2. Write out how you could think about the situation as *personal*, *permanent*, and *pervasive*.
3. Now, change your perspective: write out how the experience could be seen as *impersonal*, *impermanent*, and *specific*.
4. Try the same exercise, in reverse order, focusing on a positive event that is happening now.

---

24   Ibid.
25   Ibid.

Here is an example of how someone might change their perspective of a job loss.

Personal	Permanent	Pervasive
I am not good enough.	I will never get a job.	I am a failure at everything I do.
Impersonal	**Impermanent**	**Specific**
There is an economic downturn.	I will get a job soon.	This situation only applies to my job, not other aspects of my life.

A **growth mindset** also plays an important role in how we respond to difficult situations. A growth mindset is the belief that our abilities are malleable, like a muscle that grows and strengthens with practice. There is considerable evidence demonstrating that a growth mindset influences our persistence in the face of challenges.[26] When we have a growth mindset, we believe that our abilities reflect skills that must be learned and practiced. As a result, we remain steadfast in our purpose, confront challenges, and devote more time and effort to achieving our goals. At the same time, we accept constructive feedback, learn from our mistakes, and persevere despite failure. As a result, those with a growth mindset reach higher goals and attainments, even compared to people with similar abilities and levels of intelligence.

> When we have a growth mindset, we can reach higher goals and attainments, even compared to people with similar abilities and levels of intelligence.

A fixed mindset, conversely, is when we believe that our abilities are set. In other words, we might improve slightly, but that is about it. Our feelings of being efficacious plummet when we encounter problems, our thinking becomes more erratic, we lower our aspirations, and we put forth less effort. This

---

26 A. Bandura, "Perceived self-efficacy in cognitive development and functioning," *Educational Psychologist*, 28(2) (1993): 117–148.

is a self-fulfilling prophecy because when we put in less effort, we tend to do poorly, which reinforces our fixed mindset. When we have a fixed mindset, we are also highly sensitive to negative feedback, as we believe that any mistake is a reflection of our own self-worth. Perhaps even more important than our innate talents and abilities, it is our beliefs about the nature of learning, growth, and development that influence whether we stretch to reach our potential or accept whatever is within easy reach of our grasp.

A Jewish perspective reflects a growth mindset. In Judaism, we are taught that we must earn our own capabilities in this world. As our Sages state: "If a person says I have worked hard but have not found [success], don't believe him. [If a person says] I have not exerted myself, and I have found [success], don't believe him. [If he says] I gave it my all and I have found [success], believe him!"[27]

We are bestowed with God-given talents, intellect, and abilities. However, these are not really ours—until we deserve them. To inspire us, God often gives us a sense of our own capabilities. We might enjoy the complimentary gift but wonder: "What did I do to deserve this, and am I worthy of the responsibility that comes with this gift?" *Pirkei Avos* teaches us: "According to the labor is the reward."[28] If someone exerts little effort for something but receives praise for its accomplishment nonetheless, it can lead to low self-esteem and worthlessness. As a result, obstacles are put in our path, giving us the opportunity to become worthy of these blessings through our own hard work. When we finally arrive at some destination that we have been striving to reach, it is a sweet moment of completion: a graduation ceremony, the *chuppah*, or a child's birth. These moments are even more precious when they have been particularly challenging: graduating in the face of learning difficulties, finding your soul mate after searching for many years, or having a child after a long struggle with infertility. Our greatest accomplishments are those for which we fought to achieve. Through our own efforts, we now merit what is meant to be ours in the first place.

---

27   *Megillah* 6b.
28   *Pirkei Avos* 5:23.

According to the Vilna Gaon, every action requires a will to precede it and the capability to realize that will.[29] God has given us free will in order for us to build up and grow into our own capabilities. While we are limited by the laws of nature and God's plan for creation, there is ample room for free choice. Although one's fortune in terms of their life span, children, and livelihood may be (largely) determined from birth, sincere effort and hard work can change a person's fortune, both in terms of their material as well as spiritual position.

> Sincere effort and hard work can change a person's fortune. As we become closer and closer to God, we can rise above our lot.

How can one change their fortune? As we become closer and closer to God, thereby enjoying a greater degree of Providence, we can rise above our lot. We become closer to God through learning Torah and performing mitzvos.[30] This enables us to transcend our finite, physical being into the infinite—imbuing the world with goodness and becoming worthy recipients of God's reward in the World to Come. We thus earn our capabilities by using our own special qualities to bring forth spiritual illumination. Notwithstanding this, what is important to remember is that our life is ultimately in God's hands, and we can be assured that He is protecting and guiding us in all our affairs.[31]

GROWTH MINDSET EXERCISE

Based on Carol Dweck's work,[32] here are a few tips to encourage a growth mindset. If applying these strategies to change your own mindset, practice by using self-talk, either aloud or silently (examples are shown in parentheses).

- Understand the plasticity of the brain. Plasticity is the capacity of the brain to change with learning. When people learn,

---

29   E. E. Dessler, *Strive for the Truth! Part 2*, trans. A. Carmell (Jerusalem: Feldheim, 1978), pp. 67–68.

30   E. E. Dessler, *Strive for the Truth! Part 2*, trans. A. Carmell (Jerusalem: Feldheim, 1978).

31   A. Kaplan, *The Handbook of Jewish Thought*, vol. 2 (Maznaim Publishing, 1990).

32   C. Dweck, "Carol Dweck revisits the growth mindset," *Education Week*, 35(5) (2015): 20–24.

their neurons form new connections and synapses, leading to improved intelligence over time, regardless of their age. The process of pushing through difficult problems leads to changes in our brains that make us smarter.

- Use "process-praise" to verbally acknowledge effort rather than ability. "Process-praise" focuses on the process and emphasizes how hard work and the use of effective strategies can lead to better learning.

  - If the effort was successful, offer praise focusing on the strategy used to accomplish the task. For instance, "Great job! Using those flashcards really helped you (me) to remember the information."
  - If the effort was unsuccessful, provide some reassurance and suggest trying a different strategy. For example, "It's okay if you (I) did not find the right approach this time. Let us (me) break this down into smaller steps. What would be a possible next step to confront this issue?"
  - Be careful not to focus on "just keep trying," especially if a successful outcome is tied to changing the strategy rather than mere practice.

- Avoid using the words *can't* or *don't* when it comes to capabilities. Instead use other phrases that invoke learning as a process such as:

  - "You (I) have not learned how to do that *yet*."
  - "You (I) *still* need to understand how to do that."
  - "You are (I am) working on getting that done."
  - "You are (I am) not quite managing *yet*."

- When experiencing failure, ask questions that encourage perceiving the outcome as a learning process: "Okay, what can you (I) learn from this situation? What is this teaching you (me)? What can you (I) do differently next time? How can you (I) make this better?" Be careful to ask these questions in a (self-)compassionate, nonjudgmental manner.

"A person should look for and find his good points,
so as to revive himself and come to a place of joy.
Even if he finds just a small amount of good...this
will strengthen him and he will revitalize
himself...for he has identified in himself...an aspect
of the essence of a Jew."

Rebbe Nachman of Breslov[33]

Self-compassion, which involves being kind to yourself and accepting yourself as imperfect, is an essential part of resilience. When facing a challenging situation, conceptions about ability, control, and effort are important. However, trauma is a painful and heartbreaking experience. How do you react to your own feelings of sadness, frustration, shame, and disappointment? When we are self-compassionate, we focus on our intrinsic worth as a human being[34] and emphasize our inner strength and personal growth.

Self-compassion helps us to accept ourselves as imperfect, view setbacks as part of the larger human experience, and move forward to take on new challenges.

There are three basic components to self-compassion, including:

- treating yourself with kindness rather than being self-critical and judgmental;
- viewing your experiences as part of the larger human experience rather being isolating;
- being mindful about your painful thoughts and feelings, rather than over-identifying and becoming overwhelmed with them.[35]

Research shows that self-compassion is associated with psychological well-being and increased resilience.[36] While some might worry that you

---

33   *Likutei Moharan* 282, sect. 2.
34   K. D. Neff, "The role of self-compassion in development: A healthier way to relate to one-self," *Human Development*, 52(4) (2009): 211–214.
35   K. D. Neff, "Development and validation of a scale to measure self-compassion," *Self and Identity*, 2(2003): 223–250.
36   K. D. Neff, M. R. Leary, and R. H. Hoyle, *Handbook of Individual Differences in Social Behavior*

can be too self-compassionate, undermining motivation or becoming self-indulgent, research suggests that this does not seem to be the case.[37] Rather, self-compassion is associated with greater personal initiative to make necessary life changes.[38] As self-compassionate people do not berate themselves when they fail, they are more equipped to accept failure, adjust their tactics, and take on new challenges.[39]

Judaism emphasizes the importance of compassion and mercy. The Jewish High Holy days exemplify these beliefs in relation to our Creator. Rosh Hashanah is the day of judgment, commemorating the day that Adam was created. On this day, we reflect and evaluate our past year, but we also face forward and consider how we want to transform ourselves in the upcoming year. This day challenges us to rise above our comfort zone and connect to who we want to become. As the shofar blasts, we hear its resounding call from within us. It awakens us and brings us clarity. We are reminded that each person has the capability to positively influence the world now and in the future. Our challenge, therefore, is to fulfill our potential in this world through our own exertion.

On Yom Kippur, we reflect on our past year, both our good deeds and our misdeeds. We acknowledge our failings. Yom Kippur is not about feeling guilty, sinful, or bad. Sure, we may have made mistakes and strayed off the path, but we are not bad. Rather, we merely have forgotten who we truly are, which is fundamentally good. As *Ramban* says, "He who bestows good on his own soul is a man of loving-kindness." According to Rabbi Dessler, this statement refers to one's self-compassion for their higher self, in other words, our *neshamah*.[40]

(New York: Guilford Press, 2009) pp. 561–573; Kristin D. Neff and Pittman McGehee, "Self-compassion and Psychological Resilience Among Adolescents and Young Adults," *Self and Identity*, 9(3) (2010): 225–240.

37   K. D. Neff, "The role of self-compassion in development: A healthier way to relate to one-self," *Human Development*, 52(4) (2009): 211–214.

38   Ibid.

39   Ibid.

40   E. E. Dessler, *Strive for the Truth! Part 2*, trans. A. Carmell (Jerusalem: Feldheim, 1978).

During this time, we are focused on *teshuvah*, which means "to return" to being who we truly are, which is like God. We are taught that each of us is created in God's image and goodness is at the core of our being.[41] This is empowering, as it conveys God's belief in our intrinsic goodness and reignites our passion and purpose. We say *viduy* (confession), which expresses our regret for mistaken acts or habits, understanding that these actions do not constitute who we truly are as human beings. In *viduy*, the community recites a list of different transgressions we have committed, from *aleph* to *tav*. As we strike our chests, we reflect on our transgressions, as individuals and as part of the larger community. *Viduy* is recited in plural, as no single person has likely committed all of these sins, reminding us that we are collectively responsible for one another. Throughout our prayers, it is reiterated that God shows un-wavering compassion and mercy toward us, despite our misdeeds. Once we sincerely reflect on our behavior, we are given a clean slate, so to speak. This fresh start paves the way for renewed positive growth and personal improvement.

SELF-COMPASSION EXERCISE

These self-compassion exercises have been adapted from those sug-gested by Kristin Neff:[42]

- Consider yourself as you would a good friend. If your friend were experiencing a similar situation, what would you say? What words of comfort would you provide? Say these words aloud to yourself. You may even choose to write them down.
- Keep a (self-compassionate) journal. Write down the day's events and focus on being nonjudgmental and non-critical of yourself. Consider how your actions connect you to others and how you can learn from today for a better tomorrow.

---

41   *Bereishis* 1:27.
42   https://self-compassion.org/category/exercise/#exercise.

Here are some other ways that you can show (self-)compassion.

- Practice positive self-talk. Our internal dialogue plays an important role in how we feel about ourselves and vice versa. Be in tune
  with your inner voice. Notice when you are being overly hard on
  yourself and replace self-criticism with compassionate self-talk.
  When you make a mistake, have a conversation with yourself
  about what you have learned and avoid self-recrimination. Shift
  your self-talk to reflect a positive, encouraging, and supportive
  mindset. Be careful about how you talk aloud about yourself
  too. The outlook of your loved ones (especially children) will be
  influenced by how you speak about yourself in front of them.
- Model compassion and empathy. If your loved one experiences
  something hurtful, either emotionally or physically, acknowledge their pain. "I can see that your brother hurt your feelings
  by calling you that name. I'm sorry that happened to you. It also
  hurts my feelings when someone calls me a name. But I know
  usually they don't mean it. They just said it because they are also
  feeling hurt or angry about something."
- Remember that God created us, and we are spiritual beings. You
  are much more than your physical presence. God has mercy on
  and compassion for us. Do your best to emulate your Creator.

Self-Regulation

Self-regulation reflects the ability to control our own emotions,
thoughts, and actions and plays a key role in how we respond to stressful
and emotive events. Judaism emphasizes that we have control of our
emotions, thoughts, and actions, and that we choose whether (or not!)
to direct these toward a higher spiritual purpose. *Rambam* reiterates
this fundamental aspect of Judaism: "Every man...alone, of his own
free will, with the consent of his mind, bends to any path he may desire
to follow."[43] Nonetheless, our ancient texts are clear that our choices

---

43   *Ramban, Mishneh Torah,* Repentance 5:2.

should take the form of mitzvos. The Torah not only commands our beliefs, practices, and rituals but also instructs us on how we should act and respond emotionally to people and situations. These instructions include those that are prescribed, such as "Love your neighbor as yourself," which means that we must think and behave toward others in ways that we would want others to think and behave toward us, and those that are prohibited, such as "Do not take revenge and do not bear a grudge against your neighbor," which means that we must forgive others and seek compromise.[44] In both of these examples, there is a clear link between our thoughts and actions, which mutually reinforce each other.

Rabbi Dessler provides the following guidance: "One way to gain an inner awareness of the Creator is to train yourself to act *as if* you were on this level. Even though you are starting off with just external behavior, this will eventually have a positive influence on your inner feelings."[45] This statement further exemplifies that we have the power to transform our thoughts and emotions through our actions. When this is done in a spiritual manner, we are able to elevate ourselves and become closer to God.

When facing a difficult or challenging situation, we choose how to respond. Whether we purposely regulate our response to maximize the best outcome or we react instinctively based on our primal emotions (such as fear) makes a big difference to our resilience. Researchers have categorized different regulatory strategies that people use to cope with stressful situations.[46] These are usually conceptualized as either **active coping** or **avoidant coping**.

- Active coping involves purposefully choosing strategies that are most effective for the situation at hand.
- Avoidant coping involves attempts to deny, avoid, or disengage from stressful situations.[47]

44   *Vayikra* 19:18.

45   Zelig Pliskin, *Consulting the Wise* (Benei Yakov Publications: New York, 1991) p. 218.

46   R. S. Lazarus and S. Folkman, "Coping and adaptation," *The Handbook of Behavioral Medicine* (1984), pp. 282–325.

47   S. Folkman and J. T. Moskowitz, "Coping: Pitfalls and Promise," *Annual Review of Psychology*, 55(2004): 745–774.

These are further categorized into **problem-focused** or **emotion-focused** strategies.

- Problem-focused strategies aim to solve the challenge and do something to diminish the source of stress. These include problem-solving, planning, information-seeking, and acceptance (active) and distraction and disengagement (avoidant).

- Emotion-focused strategies aim to regulate emotions, in terms of reducing emotional distress and increasing positive emotions. These include reframing, generating positive emotions, mindfulness (active) and rumination, venting emotions, distraction, and denial (avoidant).

As one might expect, active coping leads to better outcomes in adults and children.[48] While avoidant strategies can sometimes be beneficial in the short-term, they are generally unhelpful in the long run. For example, reflecting on our emotions may help us to understand our feelings, but this can lead to ruminating (over-focusing and obsessing on past events or situations).[49] When we ruminate, our thinking becomes stuck on a track; we become so preoccupied with our negative thoughts—previous mistakes, perceived slights from other people, actions taken or not taken, imagined doomsday scenarios, opportunities lost—that we cannot push forward out of this destructive cycle. In this negative frame of mind, we interpret past events and current situations in a pessimistic light, which can lead to shame, anger, regret, envy, and feelings of hopelessness about the future.[50]

In another example, venting or expressing negative emotions may be cathartic, but long-term use of this strategy hinders the resolution of

---

48   A. T. Clarke, "Coping with interpersonal stress and psychosocial health among children and adolescents: A meta-analysis," *Journal of Youth and Adolescence*, 35(1) (2006): 10–23; J. A. Penley, J. Tomaka, and J. S. Wiebe, "The association of coping to physical and psychological health outcomes: A meta-analytic review," *J. Behav. Med.* 25(2002): 551–603.

49   D.Querstret and M. Cropley, "Assessing treatments used to reduce rumination and/or worry: A systematic review," *Clinical Psychology Review*, 33(8) (2013): 996–1009.

50   S. Nolen-Hoeksema, B. E. Wisco, and S. Lyubomirsky, "Rethinking rumination," *Perspectives on Psychological Science*, 3(5) (2008): 400–424.

a serious problem.[51] The trouble with venting is that it is a negative reinforcement process; when we express our negative emotions, we feel even more anxious and stressed.[52] Most of the time, our negative emotions would dissipate more quickly without venting and instead controlling and redirecting them toward a healthier outlet.[53]

In a final example, the use of distraction such as browsing social media, watching movies, or turning to work can take our mind off a stressful situation, but it can also prevent us from true recovery.[54] Healthy distractions can ease our pain and help us feel better but they are not a permanent solution to life's problems.

Active problem-focused coping is generally seen as the most effective way of coping with a challenging situation. It is especially advantageous to consider which specific problem-focused strategy fits with the nature of the stressful event. One important consideration is the degree of control we have over the situation.[55] When faced with a situation in which we have some measure of control, research finds it is adaptive to use **problem-solving**, **planning**, and **information-seeking** coping strategies.[56]

---

51   C. S. Carver, "Resilience and thriving: Issues, models, and linkages," *Journal of Social Issues*, 54(2) (1998): 245–266.

52   B. O. Olatunji, J. M. Lohr, and B. J. Bushman, "The pseudopsychology of venting in the treatment of anger: Implications and alternatives for mental health practice," in T. A. Cavell and K. T. Malcolm, eds., *Anger, aggression and interventions for interpersonal violence* (Lawrence Erlbaum Associates Publishers, 2007), pp. 119–141.

53   Ibid.

54   S. Najmi and D. M. Wegner, "Mental control: Thought suppression and psychopathology," *Handbook of Approach and Avoidance Motivation* (2008), pp. 447–459.

55   R. S.Lazarus and S. Folkman, *Stress, Appraisal, and Coping* (Springer Publishing Company, 1984).

56   A. T. Clarke, "Coping with interpersonal stress and psychosocial health among children and adolescents: A meta-analysis," *Journal of Youth and Adolescence*, 35(1) (2006): 10–23; J. A. Penley, J. Tomaka, J. S. Wiebe, "The association of coping to physical and psychological health outcomes: A meta-analytic review," *Journal of Behavioral Medicine*, 25 (2002), pp. 551–603; M. Zeidner and D. Saklofske, "Adaptive and maladaptive coping," in M. Zeidner and N. S. Endler, eds., *Handbook of Coping: Theory, Research, and Applications* (Wiley: Oxford, England, 1996), pp. 505–531.

- Problem-solving involves defining a problem; determining the cause of the problem; and identifying, prioritizing, selecting, and implementing a solution.[57]
- Planning includes making a plan of action and strategizing how best to proceed.[58]
- Information-seeking incorporates asking for advice and talking to people to gather more information about the situation.[59]

When faced with a situation that is out of our control, the most appropriate active problem-focused coping strategy may be **acceptance**.

- **Acceptance** acknowledges the uncontrollability of an adverse situation, helping us to focus on those aspects of life that *can* be changed.

PROBLEM-SOLVING EXERCISE

The right strategies are important to problem-solve effectively. Problem-solving is a teachable skill, which works well on your own or with another person when brainstorming together. If you are problem-solving with a child, they might contribute with drawings or whatever is most age-appropriate. If it is safe to do so, allow the child to experience the natural consequences of their actions. These consequences can be discussed and used to facilitate greater problem-solving skills in the future.

Problem-solving is a teachable skill, which works well on your own or with another person when brainstorming together.

When you have a problem or someone approaches you with a problem that needs to be dealt with, follow these steps. It is preferable to write down the solutions and their pros and cons on paper.

1. Define the problem. Make sure that you understand the problem, focusing on the causes, not the symptoms. For example,

---

57   C. S. Carver, M. F. Scheier, and J. K. Weintraub, "Assessing coping strategies: a theoretically based approach." *Journal of Personality and Social Psychology*, 56(2) (1989): 267.

58   Ibid.

59   Ibid.

the problem may be that you come home from work feeling tense. However, this may be a symptom of a different problem, such as having a stressful and long commute home from work.

2. Focus on those aspects of the problem that are solvable and have a practical solution. In the example of the stressful and long commute from work, you may not be able to change the length of your commute, but you can consider how you might make the commute more enjoyable.

3. Write down five to ten different solutions. Consider any and all possible solutions, even those that seem unlikely. Try to think outside of the box.

4. List the pros and cons of each solution. Write down the positive and negative aspects of each solution, focusing on the ease/ difficulty of implementing the solution and what might be the short- and long-term (intended and unintended) consequences.

5. Weigh each solution with its pros and cons and choose one. You may choose a solution that has the least possible changes for the greatest gain or one that has the best long-term consequences.

6. Test the solution. Give the solution a test-run and evaluate the outcome. If the solution does not seem to be working, then consider whether you wish to try another solution at the same time or abandon the first solution for a different one.

PLANNING EXERCISE

Planning is a good way to define your goals, as well as take steps toward their achievement. Below is an outline of steps to plan effectively. Write down the following steps to make them more concrete.

1. Pinpoint your goal.
2. Identify why this goal is important and meaningful to you.
3. Break down your goal into a series of smaller, feasible, and well-defined steps. Using the SMART method, the steps should be:

- Specific
- Measurable
- Attainable
- Realistic
- Time-Bound

An example of a SMART goal would be to "walk four miles on Monday from 9–10 a.m. in the park" or to "call two realtors on Tuesday morning from 10–11 a.m. to inquire about selling the house."

4. Make a chart that shows your progress toward achieving your goal.

Active emotion-focused strategies have also been shown to be effective in dealing with a stressful circumstance, either controllable or uncontrollable, and in conjunction with an active problem-focused coping strategy. The most well-researched is reframing, which is a technique that helps us to change the way in which we view a situation. Reframing involves reassessing an adverse or traumatic event and reframing its emotional impact.

There are two types of reframing:

- **Positive reframing** increases our positive emotions by reassessing a difficult situation in a positive light.
- **Negative reframing** decreases our negative emotions by reducing the negative effects of a difficult situation.[60]

Positive reframing is when we consider any potential benefits or personal growth that may result from a stressful experience. For example, when facing a divorce, one might reframe the divorce as an opportunity to find true love, increasing positive emotions.

Negative reframing is when we consider what might diminish the deleterious impact of a challenging circumstance. For instance, one

60   I. B. Mauss and M. Tamir, "Emotion goals: How their content, structure, and operation shape emotion regulation," in J. J. Gross (Ed.), *Handbook of Emotion Regulation* (2nd ed.), (New York, NY: Guilford Press, forthcoming).

might reframe a divorce as a reprieve from continued unhappiness in a marriage, reducing negative emotions.

Both positive and negative reframing have been shown to be helpful in reducing the negative consequences of a stressful situation.[61] Positive reframing, however, appears to have

> Reframing an adverse event in a positive light boosts our resilience.

longer-term positive effects on resilience.[62] Positive reframing may also boost other important active emotion-focused strategies, such as seeking emotional support, which involves talking to someone about your feelings and receiving sympathy and understanding from that person.[63]

REFRAMING EXERCISE

In the Mishnah, the ability to develop a positive outlook is referred to as an *ayin tovah*, which literally means "a good eye." The significance of *ayin tovah* means we can train ourselves to see the good. Here is a sequence of five steps (called ABCDE) that you can follow to positively reframe a stressful situation.[64] These are based on Albert Ellis's ABC model of rational emotional therapy.[65] As with all of these exercises, it is best to write these steps down.

- **Adversity.** Identify the stressful situation. For example, "My boss just told me that I have to present the bid for the new account in three days."
- **Beliefs.** Write down your pessimistic beliefs about this situation. For instance, "I don't think I will do a good job at the

---

61   G. A. Bonanno, "Loss, trauma, and human resilience: Have we underestimated the human capacity to thrive after extremely aversive events?" *American Psychologist*, 59(1) (2004): 20.

62   K. McRae and I. B. Mauss, "Increasing positive emotion in negative contexts: Emotional consequences, neural correlates, and implications for resilience," *Positive Neuroscience* (2016): 159–174.

63   C. S. Carver, M. F. Scheier, and J. K. Weintraub, "Assessing coping strategies: a theoretically based approach," *Journal of Personality and Social Psychology*, 56(2) (1989): 267.

64   M. E. Seligman, *Authentic happiness* (New York: Free Press, 2002).

65   A. Ellis, "The revised ABC's of rational-emotive therapy (RET)," *Journal of Rational-Emotive and Cognitive-Behavior Therapy*, 9(3) (1991): 139–172.

presentation. I worry that I will say the wrong thing and I cannot speak clearly."

- **C**onsequences: Consider the consequences of these pessimistic beliefs, for instance, "I am not getting anything done. I feel so nervous. I am preventing myself from moving ahead at work."

- **D**ispute: Challenge these pessimistic beliefs by remembering difficult situations that you overcame in the past. Consider five or more disputations for these negative beliefs. You may turn to a loved one if you are having difficulty with this step. For example, "This is my third presentation. The last two went well. I received good feedback from both. My boss would not have asked me to present again if she were unhappy with my presentational style. Maybe I am not giving myself enough credit. I can practice before the presentation and I am sure it will go well."

- **E**nergized and Optimistic: Use the disputations to positively reframe your original negative thoughts, which will help you feel more energized and optimistic. For example, "I feel much better now. I am able to focus on writing the presentation and I plan to practice tomorrow with my colleague."

The ability to generate **positive emotions** such as joy, contentment, love, awe, amusement, optimism, curiosity, happiness, gratitude, and interest is also considered a fundamental strength and central to human resilience and flourishing. In stressful situations, negative emotions such as fear and anger are abundant, prompting us to make quick and decisive actions (escape, attack, or push away). These momentary decisions are usually helpful in life-threatening situations (fight-or-flight), but they are counterproductive when facing serious situations that require a more nuanced and carefully planned response.

Positive emotions allow us to build on our personal resources and consider more creative and flexible ways of thinking and acting.

Positive emotions have the opposite effect on our thoughts and actions. According to the broaden-and-build theory, positive emotions broaden our momentary responses, allowing us to build on our personal resources and consider more creative and flexible ways of thinking and acting.[66] Positive emotions encourage us to play and explore, consider different perspectives and take in new information, think outside of the box, and hope and aspire for the future. Positive emotions not only make our lives more enjoyable, they also aid our emotional and physical recovery.[67] Regaining and maintaining positive emotions when faced with a stressful life experience (via having fun, laughing, and coping with humor) help to build our resilience.[68]

Although positive emotions seem incompatible with intense suffering, research finds that this is not the case.[69] Robust evidence has shown that positive emotions can co-occur with negative emotions during extremely stressful situations, often frequently.[70] In the September 11th terrorist attacks, for example, experiences of positive emotions were documented, alongside negative emotions such as fear, anger, and sadness.[71]

Research has further shown that positive emotions may correct or undo the aftereffects of lingering negative emotions, called the undoing hypothesis.[72] A positive emotion may loosen the hold that a negative emotion has on a person's mind and body and speed their recovery.

66   B. L. Fredrickson, "The role of positive emotions in positive psychology: The broaden-and-build theory of positive emotions," *American Psychologist*, 56(3) (2001): 218–226.

67   Ibid.; S.Lyubomirsky and M. D. Della Porta, "Boosting happiness, buttressing resilience: Results from cognitive and behavioral interventions, " in: J. W. Reich, A. J. Zautra, J. S. Hall, eds., *Handbook of Adult Resilience* (New York: Guilford Press, 2010), pp. 450–464.

68   J. Hutchinson and J. C. Lema, "Ordinary and extraordinary narratives of heroism and resistance: Uncovering resilience, competence and growth," *Counselling Psychology Review*, 24(3–4) (2009): 9–15.

69   S. Folkman and J. T. Moskowitz, "Positive affect and the other side of coping," *American Psychologist*, 55(6) (2000): 647–654.

70   S. Folkman, "The case for positive emotions in the stress process," *Anxiety, Stress, and Coping*, 21(1) (2008): 3–14.

71   L. Saad, "Americans anxious, but holding their heads high: Have increased confidence in government leaders, the economy," Gallup news service (2001), as cited in B. L. Fredrickson, M. M. Tugade, C. E. Waugh, and G. R. Larkin, "What good are positive emotions in crises? A prospective study of resilience and emotions following the terrorist attacks on the United States on September 11th, 2001," *Journal of Personality and Social Psychology*, 84(2) (2003): 365–376.

72   B. L. Fredrickson and R. W. Levenson, "Positive emotions speed recovery from the cardiovascular sequelae of negative emotions," *Cognition & Emotion*, 12(2) (1998): 191–220.

For example, a study of US college students' emotional responses to September 11th found that those who experienced positive emotions in the wake of the attacks such as gratitude, interest, and love were less likely to experience depression later. People who experienced positive emotions after the attacks were also found to emerge from their anguish more satisfied with life, optimistic, and tranquil than before.[73]

Positive emotions also enhance other key personal resources of resilience. Positive emotions encourage positive reframing and vice versa.[74] Positive reframing triggers positive emotions, while positive emotions increase the likelihood of finding positive meaning in subsequent stressful events. These suspected reciprocal relations suggest that the effects of positive emotions accumulate over time.[75] Positive emotions facilitate more positive coping, and this improved coping predicts future positive emotions.[76] As this upward spiral continues, people can build up their resources for resilience, which further enhance their emotional well-being.[77]

Psychological research suggests that the relationship between positive reframing and positive emotions may also be enriched through religious beliefs and practices.[78] For example, a study of 616 American Catholics, Israeli Jews, and Muslim Turks found that people who were higher in religiosity were more likely to use reframing and acceptance and less likely to engage in rumination than those who were lower in religiosity.[79] Another study of 288 Israeli Jewish and 277 American Catholic adults

73   B. L. Fredrickson, M. M. Tugade, C. E. Waugh, and G. R. Larkin, "What good are positive emotions in crisis? A prospective study of resilience and emotions following the terrorist attacks on the United States on September 11th, 2001," *Journal of Personality and Social Psychology*, 84(2) (2003): 365.

74   M. M. Tugade and B. L. Fredrickson, "Regulation of positive emotions: Emotion regulation strategies that promote resilience," *Journal of Happiness Studies*, 8(3) (2007): 311–333.

75   B. L. Fredrickson, "The role of positive emotions in positive psychology: The broaden-and-build theory of positive emotions," *American Psychologist*, 56(3) (2001): 218.

76   B. L. Fredrickson and T. Joiner, "Positive emotions trigger upward spirals toward emotional well-being," *Psychological Science*, 13(2) (2002): 172–175.

77   Ibid.

78   Ibid.

79   A. Vishkin, P. Ben-Nun Bloom, S. H. Schwartz, N. Solak, and M. Tamir, "Religiosity and Emotion Regulation," *Journal of Cross-Cultural Psychology*, 50(9) (2019): 1050–1074.

found that those who reported greater religiosity reported more fre-quent use of reframing which, in turn, was associated with more positive emotions and greater life satisfaction.[80] This finding was shown for both religious groups, even when examined separately.

Overall, these studies suggest that religion encourages people to reap-praise emotional events in a positive light which, in turn, cultivates more positive emotions and emotional well-being. As these are dynamic pro-cesses that mutually reinforce each other over time, this may encourage greater sustained protection against stressful life events in the future.

LAUGHTER EXERCISE

Laughter is often seen as the best medicine. Laughter makes us feel happy and connects us with others, both of which impacts our resilience. Laughter also enhances our learning by attracting and sustaining our attention, reducing our feelings of anxiety, and increasing our moti-vation.[81] The Talmud notes the teaching practice of the Rabbah, who, "before he began teaching halachah (law) to the Sages, he would say something humorous, and the Sages would be cheered."[82] This imparts the wisdom that one must be joyful before teaching and learning a com-plex and serious subject.

The use of laughter and humor therapy has become quite popular, which involves inducing laughter that is either humorous (spontaneous and genuine) or non-humorous (self-induced and simulated). A review of studies examining the effects of laughter-inducing therapy found that non-humorous laughter reduced feelings of depression, anxiety, depression, and physical pain.[83]

Here are a few laughter exercises that will hopefully bring a smile to your face. You can do them with another person (laughter is contagious,

---

80   Ibid.
81   B. M. Savage, H. L. Lujan, R. R. Thipparthi, and S. E. DiCarlo, "Humor, laughter, learning, and health! A brief review," *Advances in Physiology Education*, 41(3) (2017): 341–347.
82   *Shabbos* 30b.
83   C. N. Van der Wal and R. N. Kok, "Laughter-inducing therapies: Systematic review and meta-analysis," *Social Science & Medicine* (2019).

after all) or on your own. Self-induced laughter is fine. Whether genuine or not, laughter still has benefits! Do your best to act happy and joyful, move around energetically, and focus on the moment.

> Whether genuine or not, laughter still has benefits!

A laughter session typically has three stages. For each stage, choose one or two of these exercises.[84]

1. Opening and warming up. *Grateful laughter*: Spread your arms up, laugh straight from your heart, bring the arms down, and then raise them again. *Wild laughter*: Howl, growl, and make animal sounds. *Vowel laughter*: Laugh using different vowels and sounds (hehe, haha, heeho, heehaa, heehohoo). *Humming laughter*: Laugh with your mouth closed and hum your favorite tune. *Gradient laughter*: Smile slowly, giggle, laugh softly, gradually increasing in your tempo and volume. *Clapping*: Clap your hands in rhythm while chanting, "ho ho ha ha ha."

2. Experiencing positive emotions, humor, and laughter. *Flying bird*: Flap your arm and run around laughing. *Regal laughter*: Walk like a king/queen, pretending you are between rows of applauding subjects. *Hugging laughter*: Hug and laugh. *Laughter sneeze*: Sneeze and laugh (achoo achoo, haha haha). *Touch the sky laughter*: Make a big circle and hold hands with a few others. Run toward the center of the circle while shouting and extending your arms. Burst out laughing, looking up when you reach the center. *Lion laughter*: Before a mirror, open your mouth wide, stick out your tongue, lift up your hands as if they were paws, and roar, laughing like a lion.

3. Recovery and closure. *Silent laughter*: Be completely still and silent while sitting or lying down, eyes closed, and let any laughter come out freely. *Laughter meditation*: Sit or lie on the floor in stillness and silence. Be mindful of how your body feels and what thoughts and emotions arise.

---

84   R. Mora-Ripoll, "Simulated laughter techniques for therapeutic use in mental health," *Journal of Psychology & Clinical Psychiatry*, 8(2) (2017):00479.

GRATITUDE EXERCISE

Gratitude is the first word on our lips in the morning and linked to our identity as Jews. When we wake up in the morning while still in bed, "*Modeh*" (give thanks) is the first word we say, before we say "*ani*" (I). The fourth son of Yaakov and Leah was named Yehudah, whose name can be translated as "thanks." From the kingdom of Yehudah, the name Jew (Yehudi) was derived.

One way we can practice gratitude is with this exercise. In an online intervention, those who engaged in this exercise were happier and less depressed six months later compared to a group who did not do the exercise.[85]

- Every night, set aside five to ten minutes before you go to sleep. Using a notebook or journal, write down the following:
  - Three things that went well today. These can be trivial but must be significant to you. For example, "My spouse brought me flowers."
  - Next to each positive event, answer the question, Why did this happen? For example, "My husband is very thoughtful" or "He wanted to make me happy for Shabbos."

Some other ways to express gratitude include:

- For younger children, you can use a similar strategy to the three things listed above, focusing on one or two things and discussing this as a conversation before bedtime.
- Say "*Baruch Hashem*" or "Thank God" whenever you have something to be thankful for. Be careful not to say these words out of habit without conscious thought. When you say these words, verbalize aloud why you have done so. "*Baruch Hashem*, I arrived at the store five minutes before they closed."
- Before bedtime, visualize three things that happened that day when you felt gratitude for God's guidance and thank Him aloud.

---

85   M. E. Seligman, T. A. Steen, N. Park, and C. Peterson, "Positive psychology progress: empirical validation of interventions," *American Psychologist*, 60(5) (2005): 410.

Mindfulness is another self-regulatory approach that helps us to deal with stressful situations. While some researchers have focused on mindfulness as a personality trait or characteristic, it can also be conceptualized as a practice. Mindfulness practice involves intentionally focusing one's attention on the internal and external experiences happening in the present moment and is often taught through a variety of meditation exercises.[86] Mindfulness has been described as "bringing one's complete attention to the present experience on a moment-to-moment basis"[87] and as "paying attention in a particular way: on purpose, in the present moment, and nonjudgmentally."[88]

A number of studies have tested the effectiveness of mindfulness training. These have generally found that those who received the training had more positive psychological outcomes compared to those who did not receive the training. These studies focused on specific groups of people including those experiencing chronic pain, mental health problems, or stressful work environments in the military or healthcare.[89] Research has also found that mindfulness training increases the use of problem-solving coping strategies and may also reduce rumination.[90] Whether mindfulness promotes resilience when facing severe trauma is less certain. However, similar to other emotion-focused strategies, mindfulness may alleviate emotional distress associated with the trauma, allowing one to better utilize an appropriate problem-focused coping strategy for recovery.

---

86 R. A. Baer, "Mindfulness training as a clinical intervention: A conceptual and empirical review," *Clinical Psychology: Science and Practice*, 10(2) (2003): 125–143.

87 G. A. Marlatt and J. L. Kristeller, *Mindfulness and Meditation* (1999), p. 68.

88 J. Kabat-Zinn, *Wherever You Go There You Are* (New York: Hyperion, 1994), p. 4.

89 R. A. Baer, "Mindfulness training as a clinical intervention: A conceptual and empirical review," *Clinical Psychology: Science and Practice*, 10(2) (2003): 125–143; A. P. Jha, A. B. Morrison, S. C. Parker, and E. A. Stanley, "Practice is protective: Mindfulness training promotes cognitive resilience in high-stress cohorts," *Mindfulness*, 8(1) (2017): 46–58.

90 R. A. Baer, "Mindfulness training as a clinical intervention: A conceptual and empirical review," *Clinical Psychology: Science and Practice*, 10(2) (2003): 125–143; E. Halland, M. De Vibe, I. Solhaug, O. Friborg, J. H. Rosenvinge, R. Tyssen,...and A. Bjørndal, "Mindfulness training improves problem-focused coping in psychology and medical students: Results from a randomized controlled trial," *College Student Journal*, 49(3) (2015): 387–398.

A focus on the present moment coincides with the Jewish conceptualization of time. According to our Sages, each moment has a unique spiritual energy that allows us to achieve what is needed at that particular point.[91] Although events in our days, weeks, and years reoccur—for example, our daily prayers, weekly observance of Shabbos, and celebration of holidays—no two moments are identical. Rather, these moments link in a spiral, circling upward toward ever higher dimensions of spiritual growth.[92] Each moment we experience acts as a spark to ignite our ascension. It is clear that our daily lives require our full attention and focused concentration. Being mindful of the opportunities inherent in each moment enables us to move forward and actualize our spiritual potential, bringing us closer to God and the purpose of our existence.

MINDFULNESS EXERCISE

Mindfulness involves awareness of our thoughts and emotions as well as the world around us. Being mindful allows us to step back from our thinking and notice patterns that may be non-productive. For example, we may notice that we are overthinking and brooding. Being mindful, we can also notice when our thoughts are creating stress and anxiety. Such awareness can be a powerful tool in helping us to realize that we do not need to be driven or controlled by our unhelpful thoughts. Here are some recommendations on how to be more mindful.[93]

> Mindfulness is a powerful tool in helping us to realize that we do not need to be controlled by our unhelpful thoughts.

- **Notice the everyday.** As you go through your day, be aware of the sensations you experience, including the taste of food, the smell of the outdoors, the feeling of the ground beneath your feet, and the wind rushing past you.

91   A. Tatz, *Living Inspired* (New York: Targum Press, 1993).
92   Ibid.
93   Professor Mark Williams, https://www.nhs.uk/conditions/stress-anxiety-depression/mindfulness/.

- **Keep it regular.** Find a set time when you choose to be more mindful. A good time might be when you are in a pleasant and relaxing environment.
- **Try something new.** When you do something different, you might experience life in a new way. Try sitting in a different place than your usual spot, walk a new route, or taste a novel food or flavor.
- **Focus on the present.** It can be difficult to clear your mind, especially when you are still. If past worries or future plans begin to crowd into your mind, view these as mental events. You can visualize these ideas floating up in the air, represented as kites, bees, or butterflies, or driving away from you, represented as cars, motorcycles, or trains.
- **Name your feelings.** When you feel difficult emotions, ask yourself exactly what you are feeling (envy, shame, frustration, etc.). Labeling your emotions can be empowering and helps you to understand their purpose. Our emotions offer insight into who we are and what we want to change.
- **Free yourself from negative thinking.** Mindfulness can help you if you are stuck in negative thought patterns such as critical self-talk or catastrophizing (see exercise in family situational meanings). To counter negative thinking, use a mindfulness technique that acknowledges thoughts but then releases them. Instead of fighting with negative thoughts or suppressing them (both of which require a lot of energy!), separate yourself from them. You might, for example, open your hands and visualize these thoughts floating away. If they return, acknowledge them but then imagine releasing them again. Another option is thanking the mind. You might say, "Thank you for these thoughts, but I'll pass on them." These exercises teach us that negative thoughts come and go, but they do not have to take ahold of us. When we let them go, we make room for a more positive mindset.

In addition to these strategies, you may also try the following mindfulness meditation.

1. Define a time and quiet place for your practice. Wearing comfortable clothing, sit up straight but in a relaxed position. Think about what your arms are doing. Now focus on what your legs are doing. You may wish to close your eyes. Consider what is your intention at this moment.
2. Breathe deeply, inhaling slowly, then holding your breath for three seconds and exhaling slowing, then holding your breath for another three seconds. Do this for a few minutes. Focus on your breathing, but forgive yourself when your mind wanders.
3. When you are finished, open your eyes. Slowly, become aware of your present moment and surroundings.

Existential Beliefs

Research confirms that religious **faith** is important for resilience. Studies have shown that religious beliefs, in terms of faith and spirituality, help people navigate hardships during their teenage, adult, and older years.[94] While faith may help someone cope with mishaps and misfortunes (Gall et al., 2005), research finds some possible risks as well:

- Turning to faith may discourage problem-solving, as someone may wait for a solution from God rather than actively seek to resolve their own problems.[95]
- Someone may also perceive their adversity as a punishment from God, which can exacerbate feelings of guilt and shame, which in turn increase distress.[96]

---

94   J. F. Peres, A. Moreira-Almeida, A. G. Nasello, and H. G. Koenig, "Spirituality and resilience in trauma victims," *Journal of Religion and Health*, 46(3) (2007): 343–350; S. Kim and G. B. Esquivel, "Adolescent spirituality and resilience: Theory, research, and educational practices," *Psychology in the Schools*, 48(7) (2011): 755–765; L. K. Manning, "Navigating hardships in old age: Exploring the relationship between spirituality and resilience in later life," *Qualitative Health Research*, 23(4) (2013): 568–575.

95   K. I. Pargament and J. Cummings, "Anchored by faith: Religion as a resilience factor," in J. W. Reich, A. J. Zautra, J. S. Hall, eds., *Handbook of Adult Resilience* (New York, NY, US: Guilford Press, 2010), pp. 193–210.

96   Ibid.

Religious faith, on its own, may not be enough to cope with particularly challenging periods.[97] Both faith and hope are essential in managing uncertainty and coping effectively with a changing reality.[98] **Hope** is expectant and forward-looking but grounded in reality and rooted in our personal experiences.[99] Hope inspires, brings vitality, and fuels our passion for living.[100] Without hope, everything is meaningless and purposeless: our motivation and desire are absent, and we are despondent and helpless.[101] Research finds that hope is an important aspect of resilience, enabling individuals to maintain faith in their recovery.[102] Of course, faith and hope are mutually reinforcing: faith bolsters hope and vice versa.[103]

Hope is an important aspect of resilience, enabling individuals to maintain faith in their recovery.

The active expression of faith and hope is **meaning-making**. Meaning-making concerns the ultimate questions about life, its meaning, and our relationships with the sacred and transcendent. Meaning-making is focused on understanding and making sense of life events, relationships, and the self.[104] The concept of meaning-making draws on Viktor Frankl's *Man's Search for Meaning*, first published in 1946. The book describes his experiences as a Jewish prisoner in a Nazi concentration camp during World War II and his psychotherapeutic method, logotherapy, which involves identifying a unique and specific purpose in life that must and can be fulfilled by that person alone. According to

---

97   Ibid.

98   S. Folkman, "Stress, coping, and hope," *Psycho-oncology*, 19(9) (2010): 901–908.

99   D. Clarke, "Faith and hope," *Australasian Psychiatry*, 11(2) (2003): 164–168.

100   Ibid.

101   Ibid.

102   B. M. Iacoviello and D. S. Charney, "Psychosocial facets of resilience: implications for preventing posttrauma psychopathology, treating trauma survivors, and enhancing community resilience," *European Journal of Psychotraumatology*, 5(1) (2014):23970.

103   D. A. Pardini, T. G. Plante, A. Sherman, and J. E.Stump, "Religious faith and spirituality in substance abuse recovery: Determining the mental health benefits," *Journal of Substance Abuse Treatment*, 19(4) (2000): 347–354.

104   Michael Ignelzi, "Meaning-making in the learning and teaching process," *New Directions for Teaching and Learning*, (82) (Summer 2000): 5–14.

Frankl, "striving to find a meaning in one's life is the primary motivational force in man."[105]

When someone experiences a traumatic event, they may ask themselves questions such as, "What is the purpose of this event?" and "Why did this happen to me?" Meaning-making is an active coping strategy focused on understanding the greater purpose of a traumatic event.[106] Having a strong sense of meaning and purpose in life as well as attributing tragic situations to benevolent religious reasons (for example, to the will of God rather than to human error) relate to better recovery from trauma.[107]

When meaning-making, we reappraise an event to be consistent with our beliefs. When a traumatic situation is contrary to our beliefs, we need to rebuild our meaning-making systems to accommodate our understanding of the event.[108] Successful meaning-making resolves these discrepancies, restoring equilibrium between the traumatic event and our conceptualization of life's purpose and meaning. This is not an easy process, especially when an event is so distressing that it completely shatters our purposeful existence. As Viktor Frankl so aptly explains in regard to restoring a man's inner strength in the concentration camp:

> Successful meaning-making restores the equilibrium between the traumatic event and our conceptualization of life's purpose and meaning.

> *What we needed was a fundamental change in our attitude toward life. We had to learn ourselves and, furthermore, we had to teach the despairing men, that it did not really matter what we expected from life, but rather what life expected of us. We needed to stop asking the meaning of life and instead think of ourselves as those who were questioned in life—daily and*

105 V. Frankl, *Man's Search for Meaning* (London: Rider, 2004), p. 46.
106 C. L. Park, "Meaning making and resilience," in *The Routledge International Handbook of Psychosocial Resilience* (2016), pp. 162–172.
107 Ibid.
108 C. L. Park and S. Folkman, "Meaning in the context of stress and coping," *Review of General Psychology*, 1(2) (1997): 115–144.

hourly. Our answer must consist not of talk and meditation, but in the right action and in the right conduct. Life ultimately means finding the right answer to its problems and to fulfill the task it constantly sets for each individual. These tasks, and therefore, the meaning of life, differ from man to man and from moment to moment…When man finds that it is his destiny to suffer, he will have to accept his suffering as his task; his single and unique task…His unique opportunity lies in the way in which he bears his burden.[109]

For Jewish people, our most salient protective factor is our *emunah,* our faith in God. According to *Rambam, emunah* is the knowledge that God created and continues to run all of Creation. *Rambam* defines *emunah* in the first of the Thirteen Principles of Faith: "The Creator, blessed be He, created and orchestrates all activities, and He alone did, does, and will do all actions." Judaism is not based on blind faith. In other words, we do not believe everything we hear or read. Furthermore, faith is not an intellectual exercise; it does not involve propositions that we are unprepared to follow in our own lives. Rather, *Rambam* emphasizes that we *know* there is a Creator. Our faith involves only "those matters which in the depths of his heart he recognizes as true and decisive for him. It follows that the degree of a person's faith depends on the purity of his heart. Only one who is basically honest and true to himself (*ne'eman*) can be a man of faith (*maamin*)."[110] Hence, *emunah* is an innate understanding, a perception of the truth that transcends reason.

Emunah goes hand in hand with *bitachon.* The *Chovos Halevavos* defines *bitachon* as trusting God.[111] "I will say of God. He is my refuge and my fortress, my God. I will trust in Him."[112] *Bitachon* is a powerful sense of optimism and confidence that everything that God does is for the

---

109   V. Frankel, *Man's Search for Meaning* (London: Rider, 2004), pp. 85–86.

110   E. E. Dessler, *Strive for the Truth! Part 2*, trans. A. Carmell (Jerusalem: Feldheim, 1978), p. 134.

111   *Chovos Halevavos, Shaar Habitachon*, as cited by Rabbi Ben Tzion Shafier, https://www. ou.org/life/inspiration/difference-emunah-bitachon/.

112   *Tehillim* 91:2.

best. We are taught that *emunah* and *bitachon* are one and the same, with *emunah* likened to the tree and *bitachon* to the fruit.[113]

The interdependent relationship between *emunah* and *bitachon* is highlighted in the splitting of the Yam Suf. One can imagine the Jewish People, seven days after their freedom from slavery, standing at the edge of the sea. The angry and vengeful Egyptian army was advancing toward them. To the side, there were wild animals. In the sky, the angel of the Egyptians was coming to protect the Egyptians. There was nowhere to turn. Moshe said to the Jewish People, "Fear not; stand by and see the salvation of God, which He will show you today. For as you have seen Egypt this day, you shall not see them again, forever. God shall fight for you, and you shall be silent."[114] God sent a message to Moshe: "Why do you cry to me? Tell the Israelites to advance."[115] According to the midrash, no one advanced, and the sea did not part. God waited, as the first step needed to be taken by the Jewish People, and only then were they deemed worthy of the great miracle. While others stood with indecision and fear at the water's edge, Nachshon ben Aminadav, prince of the tribe of Judah and the brother-in-law of Aharon, jumped into the sea, nearly losing his life as the waters reached his mouth and nostrils.[116] Moshe then prayed, and God replied, "You lift your staff and spread your hand over the seas, which will split, and Israel will come into the sea upon dry land."[117] The sea parted, and the Jewish People entered and were saved from the Egyptian assault. After they witnessed the miracle of the splitting of the Yam Suf, the Jewish People reached such a high level of faith and trust in God that it continues to sustain us even through the most challenging times.

Nachshon's faith that God *could* part the Yam Suf and his trust that God *would* do so highlights the dynamic relationship between *emunah* and *bitachon*. Both are necessary and mutually reinforcing, especially

---

113   *Ramban* (1194–1270), *Ha'emunah V'Habitachon*, chap. 1.
114   *Shemos* 14: 13–14.
115   Ibid., 14:15.
116   M. Caminker, https://www.chabad.org/library/article_cdo/aid/2199147/jewish/Nachshon-ben-Aminadav-The-Man-Who-Jumped-Into-the-Sea.htm.
117   *Shemos* 14:16.

when facing difficulties that challenge our sense of meaning and purpose in this world and threaten our existence. Nevertheless, having *emunah* and *bitachon* does not mean that we should wait for God to resolve our problems, without any effort on our own part. Nachshon teaches us that we must move forward to receive God's help. As the saying goes, if you ask God, "Please, can I win the lottery?" you must first buy a ticket. This is the same reason that God told Noach to build a very large ark. Without a miracle, even an ark many times its size would be too small to hold everything that was supposed to go into it. So, why build such a large ark, or even build an ark at all? According to *Ramban*: Noach built a very large ark "to lessen the miracle, this is the way with all miracles…that man should do all that is humanly possible and leave the rest in the hands of Heaven."[118]

MEANING-MAKING EXERCISE

A potent factor for resilience is seeing the true nature of the world as infused with God's meaning, rather than being haphazard. Here is a set of beautiful reflections inspired by Rabbi Simcha Zissel Ziv from Kelm, which may help to increase your *emunah*.[119]

- When you experience an event, visualize in your mind the cause of that event, the cause of that cause, and so on, until you reach the Cause of all causes, our Creator.
- Reflect on the miraculous nature of every moment of life. What we experience at every second is nothing short of a miracle.
- Learn to recognize the miracles we experience on a daily basis. These are the extraordinary coincidences that occur every single day in our lives. This might include when you *happen* to see a friend in another country. When you *happen* to be sitting at the same Shabbos table with a family who *happen* to have the exact knowledge or experience that you are seeking. Or when you *happen* to hear the right *shiur* (lesson) at the right time. These

---

118 *Ramban*, commentary on *Bereishis* 6:19.
119 As cited in E. E. Dessler, *Strive for the Truth! Part 2*, trans. A. Carmell (Jerusalem: Feldheim, 1978), p. 286.

are God's ways of guiding us toward the direction that we need to go. Notice these open miracles and acknowledge their Creator.

Here is another powerful imagery inspired by Rabbi Dessler.[120] Consider using this as a meditation on your own spiritual life, which embodies your *emunah* and *bitachon*.

- Imagine yourself as a tree. Your roots are planted deep in the ground, receiving nourishment from the earth and allowing you to grow spiritually. These roots hold you firmly when your branches sway in the face of storm and turmoil. Consider what enables you to stand firm in stormy times, threatening your very existence. What provides you with strength and sustenance, and how do your actions reflect the nature of this foundation and these roots?

FAMILY STRENGTHS

The family is the basic building block of civilization and the single most important influence in many people's lives. In Judaism, the family is central. Still, how we define our family depends on our own circumstances. While the nature of a family has changed with modern society, it usually includes a group of related people who live in the same household. With divorce, remarriage, and single-parent households being more common, this can mean a number of different family combinations, with or without children.

Whatever its composition, the significance of the family cannot be overstated. For children, the family represents their first and foremost attachment. With their parents, children form a relationship that is considered the basis of all others in their lifetime. The family is where children are shown how to love, how to trust, and how to live. Through their family, children come to learn the meaning of kindness, caring, and friendship. They also understand their own self-worth, acquire their feelings of self-respect, recognize their own capabilities, and develop their aspirations. As part of a family, children are taught how

---

120 E. E. Dessler, *Strive for the Truth! Part 1*, trans. A. Carmell (Jerusalem: Feldheim, 1978), pp. 228–229.

to relate to others, what is the right way to behave, what to value, and what to believe. Parents are children's first role models and, as a result, children often replicate their parents' behaviors and reinforce their parents' (stated and unstated) beliefs and values.

Once children become teens, the family (hopefully) represents a safe place from where they can practice acting more like adults. Adolescence is a time of transition where many changes occur simultaneously, including biological changes such as puberty and brain development and social changes such as the transition to (junior) high school, the increasing importance of friends, and greater needs for autonomy and independence. This can and often does create some turbulence in family relationships; nevertheless, this conflict is usually short-lived.[121] What is important to remember is that parents still matter during the teen years (the majority of the time, anyway!). How teens mature into adults and the relationships they form are shaped by their parents, to a large degree.

As teens transition into adults, they begin to form their own serious relationships, partnerships, and families. While some consciously decide to live their lives differently from their parents, many of us are still influenced by our family of origin, for better or for worse. Nevertheless, as adults, there is freedom and flexibility to choose our own pathways and create our own families, with the hope of meeting our loftiest aspirations and ambitions of family life.

Where does one begin in fostering family resilience? As with personal strengths that imbue resilience, the essential ingredient is our Creator. From the Jewish perspective, we are taught that God is an intimate part of our relationship with our spouse and children. The Talmud says that there are three partners in the development of every child: God, the father, and the mother.[122] Similarly, God is a silent but conscious partner in marriage. The ideal marriage consists of a triangle composed

121   L. M. Gutman, S. C. Peck, O. Malanchuk, A. J. Sameroff, and J. S. Eccles, "Moving through adolescence: Developmental trajectories of African American and European American youth," *Monographs of the Society for Research in Child Development*, 82(4) (2017): 1–142.
122   *Kiddushin* 30b.

of a man, a woman, and God. Thus, our bonds with our spouses and children are spiritual ones, obligating us to nurture and respect these relationships as they are symbolic of our relationship with God. This is inspiring; we are bound to each other not only through biology and social practice but as a way of honoring and expressing our love for our Creator.

Family resilience is cultivated in the course of everyday practices that are warm and supportive—a conversation here, a mutual activity there, and a helping hand, whenever needed. Through our words, experiences, and gestures, a diverse group of individuals builds resilience together through their shared bonds. There is no single formula for family resilience. Families come in various configurations, operate according to their own values and moral codes, face their own unique challenges, and have their own set of strengths. Beyond these differences, what really matters is how families interact with one another, in terms of the love and support they share, their communication style, the structure and consistency of their home life, and their common sense of purpose and belonging. Families are similar to a tapestry, woven through generations and tied together with love and forgiveness, intimacy and independence, stability and transformation, laughter and tears.

> There is no single formula for family resilience; what really matters is how families interact with one another.

As with personal strengths, family strengths are not static qualities. Rather, they are interactional processes, which evolve over time in relation to changes within and outside of the family. They can be built up at any point in the family cycle, but they also need to be continually renewed and maintained. The necessity for renewal coincides with our relationship with God. As we say in our daily prayers, "He who in His goodness renews each day, constantly, the first act of Creation." We are taught that God perpetually and actively creates every moment, expressing His eternal love for us. In a similar sense, our spiritual relationships with our spouses and children must also be revitalized on a continual basis, reaffirming our love and commitment.

When we consider family strengths, these can be categorized according to four main goals:

- **Family relationships**: Do you have a stable family life? Are your family relationships secure and safe? Do family members freely express and receive love?
- **Family communication**: Does your family listen without judgment? Does your family share their good news, as well as their troubles? Does your family brainstorm together when problems arise?
- **Family management and organization**: Is your family life organized? Does your family follow a basic routine? Can your family manage challenges together?
- **Family meaning**: Does your family share a similar worldview? Does your family have a cohesive identity? Does your family create meaning from shared challenges?

FAMILY STRENGTHS EXERCISE

Here is a questionnaire which may help you understand your family's strengths.[123] Read each statement below and decide how often/to what degree each statement is true of your family (1 = Never, 2 = Rarely, 3 = Somewhat, 4 = Often, 5 = Almost Always). You can also ask other members of your family to answer these questions. These questions may serve as a springboard for discussion. As a family, pick out one or two areas that are strengths, as well as one or two areas that you would like to improve.

1. We enjoy talking to one another.
2. Our family recognizes when a problem exists.
3. Our family handles stress well.
4. We feel a strong connection with one another.
5. Our family can come up with solutions to resolve problems.

123   Strengthening Families Program, Cornell University, https://www.human.cornell.edu/sites/default/files/PAM/Parenting/Family%20Strengths%20Activities.pdf.

6. We discuss things before decisions are made that affect the whole family.
7. We feel comfortable sharing our affection with one another.
8. Everyone gets a say in family decisions.
9. We are respectful to one another when someone is expressing a different point of view.
10. It is easy for us to work together to overcome crises in our family.
11. Family members do not have any problems meeting their responsibilities.
12. We are sensitive to other family member's feelings.
13. We can effectively talk to one another even when we are upset.
14. We trust one another.
15. We give praise when someone has done something positive.
16. We support one another even when someone has made a bad decision.
17. When we ask someone in our family to do something, they do it.
18. We are kind to one another.
19. We have enjoyable memories with one another.
20. We do not put one another down.
21. We support family members, even when we disagree with them.
22. We often confide in one another.
23. We are committed to supporting our family's well-being.
24. Our family has fun together.

Family Relationships

"Much of resilience, especially in childhood, but also throughout the life-span, is embedded in close relationships with other people."[124]

In the family context, nothing is more important than having a **stable, safe, and nurturing relationship**. For children, this is characterized by having parents who sensitively respond to and meet the physical (food, shelter, hygiene, and medical care), emotional (affection,

---

124 S. M. Southwick, G. A. Bonanno, A. S. Masten, C. Panter-Brick, and R. Yehuda, "Resilience definitions, theory, and challenges: interdisciplinary perspectives," *European Journal of Psychotraumatology*, 5(1) (2014):25338.

empathy, acceptance, and positive affirmation), and developmental (communication, imaginative play, learning and reading, and outdoor activities) needs of the child.[125] For adults, a stable, safe, and nurturing relationship involves having an emotionally close, intimate partnership, which provides instrumental and emotional support and positive, healthy communication. As we will see below, spousal and parent-child relationships that are characterized in this manner are protective for both adults and children, having long-term implications for resilience. The degree to which a spouse interacts in nurturing ways with their partner not only promotes their partner's health and well-being, it also enhances their parenting and the home life, enabling their offspring to navigate through both calm and turbulent times.

For children, the family forms their first significant relationship. Their attachment usually begins with their mother, expanding to include the father, siblings, and other close relatives. According to attachment theory, how parents respond to their infant's needs during this period of complete dependency has a profound and lasting influence on a person's capacity to establish and maintain emotional bonds with others.[126] This dynamic process constructs a "working model" that shapes their feelings of self-worth, expectations of the world, and reactions to others. When children are securely attached to their parents, they are confident that their parents are dependable, which forms a secure base for the child to explore the world. For over fifty years, research has consistently shown that having a secure attachment, in terms of a responsive, sensitive, supportive, structured, and emotionally stimulating parent-child relationship, plays a critical role in children's positive development.[127]

---

125   Centers for Disease Control and Prevention, Strategic direction for maltreatment prevention: "Preventing child maltreatment through the promotion of safe, stable, and nurturing relationships between children and caregivers," https://www.cdc.gov/ViolencePrevention/pdf/CM_Strategic_Direction--Long-a.pdf.

126   J. Bowlby, *Attachment and Loss, Volume 1: Attachment* (New York: Basic Books, 1982).

127   L. M. Gutman and E. Flouri, "Risk and resilience in development," in Slater and Brenner, eds., *Introduction to Psychology: Third Edition* (New York, NY: Wiley-Blackwell, 2017), pp. 645–682.

The security of attachment has also been shown to differentiate between positive and negative outcomes for children exposed to stressful circumstances and trauma.[128] This is likely because having a secure relationship with parents fosters the development of important personal strengths, including feelings of self-efficacy and self-compassion, as well as active coping strategies such as problem-solving and seeking emotional support.

What children learn about the safety and security of emotional relationships during their earliest years continues to influence their outcomes throughout their lifetime. Studies examining the same group of individuals from birth to adulthood have shown that those who had secure attachments in infancy tended to have more positive relationships with their friends and romantic partners and better mental health in adulthood, while those who had insecure attachments were at greater risk of poor functioning relationships and mental health problems.[129] A secure parent-child attachment thus forms the basis for resilience both in childhood and throughout adulthood.[130]

It is important to highlight that the relationship between early attachment and later resilience is not a linear one; rather, it is a dynamic and cumulative process. In other words, the nature of our early attachment impacts how we view our environment (as safe and secure or threatening and unpredictable), which influences our social interactions, which then shape our relationships, and so forth. With this in mind, there are several points about nurturing family relationships that should be highlighted, especially in regard to fostering resilience.

First, while our attachment orientation is relatively stable throughout life, the nature of our attachment can change, becoming more or

---

128   A. S. Masten and J. D. Coatsworth, "The development of competence in favorable and unfavorable environments: Lessons from research on successful children," *American Psychologist*, 53(2) (1998): 205.

129   L. A. Sroufe, LB. Egeland, E. A. Carlson, and W. A. Collins, *The development of the person: The Minnesota Study of Risk and Adaptation from birth to adulthood* (New York: Guilford Press, 2005); J. A. Simpson, W. A. Collins, S. Tran, and K. C. Haydon, "Attachment and the experience and expression of emotions in romantic relationships: A developmental perspective," *Journal of Personality and Social Psychology*, 92(2) (2007): 355–367.

130   Ibid.

less secure, based on our relationship experiences.[131] There is strong evidence that, for example, parents can improve their interactions with their children which, in turn, enhances their attachment.[132] Parents can be taught to be more sensitive and responsive to their children through video feedback, which involves videotaping a parent-child interaction in the home environment and then providing constructive feedback on the parent's behavior. Conversely, research also suggests that children can experience a change from being secure to insecure, especially in the context of an adverse event such as a divorce or bereavement.[133] As adults, our "working model" of relationships can also be updated and revised in light of our new relationships. We might, for example, become more secure in a loving, stable marriage, while an abusive relationship might lead us from being secure to insecure, mistrusting others and doubting ourselves.

Second, in light of the first point, our relationships with parents, spouses, children, and other loved ones require nurturing on a continual basis. Nurturing is expressed as positive time spent together, interacting and communicating in ways that are responsive, accepting, affirming, empathetic, and growth orientated. Nurturing also involves affectionate touch. Research highlights the importance of touch for both children and adults. Studies have shown that affectionate touching—such as handholding and hugging—has positive physiological and biochemical effects and is a vital part of our social interactions with loved ones.[134] For example, a warm hug with a loved one has been shown

131 W. J. Chopik, R. S. Edelstein, and K. J. Grimm, "Longitudinal changes in attachment orientation over a 59-year period," *Journal of Personality and Social Psychology*, 116(4) (2019): 598–611.

132 M. J. Bakermans-Kranenburg, M. H. Van Ijzendoorn, and F. Juffer, "Less is more: meta-analyses of sensitivity and attachment interventions in early childhood," *Psychological Bulletin*," 129(2) (2003): 195–215.

133 B. Egeland and E. A. Carlson, "Attachment and psychopathology," *Attachment Issues in Psychopathology and Intervention* (2004): 27–48; M. Lewis, C. Feiring, and S. Rosenthal, "Attachment over time," *Child Development*, 71(3) (2000): 707–720.

134 T. Field, "Touch for socioemotional and physical well-being: A review," *Developmental Review*, 30(4) (2010): 367–383.

to lower the heart rate and blood pressure.[135] For spouses, examples of nurturing might include spontaneously sending a special note/message expressing appreciation, offering to do an important errand, spending alone time together, asking about and discussing daily events, and providing physical affection that is nurturing, such as a light touch on the shoulder, embrace, or kiss on the cheek. For children, examples of nurturing might include reading books together regularly at bedtime, going for walks and letting the child steer the conversation, positively engaging in projects and homework together, consistently offering words of praise and encouragement, and giving affection even to older children and teens.

There is some disagreement about whether it is the quantity or quality of the time spent together that matters most in a relationship. In either case, what seems to be important is that these interactions transmit love, nurturance, and support from partner to partner and from parent to child.[136] Given the increasing demands on modern life, researchers suggest that those everyday activities that are often plentiful, such as doing household chores and running errands, provide opportunities for spontaneous moments of togetherness, which are nurturing when shared in an affirmative and enjoyable manner.[137]

Third, the importance of the father's role in nurturing family relationships should not be underplayed. Although traditionally most of the research has focused on mothers, there is increasing evidence that fathers, whether living or not in the residential home, count too.[138] Fathers have a key influence on children's outcomes—including their resilience in times of

> Fathers play a critical role in ensuring a secure attachment.

135   K. M. Grewen, B. J. Anderson, S. S. Girdler, and K. C. Light, "Warm partner contact is related to lower cardiovascular reactivity," *Behavioral Medicine*, 29(3) (2003): 123–130.

136   R. E. Larson and M. H. Richards, *Divergent realities: The emotional lives of mothers, fathers, and adolescents* (New York: Basic Books, 1994).

137   T. Kremer-Sadlik and A. L. Paugh, "Everyday Moments: Finding quality time in American working families," *Time & Society*, 16(2–3) (2007): 287–308.

138   B. Featherstone, "Fathers matter: A research review," *Children & Society*, 18(4) (2004): 312–319.

adversity.[139] Fathers often provide a different but complementary style of nurturing than mothers, such as engaging in rough-and-tumble play and encouraging risk-taking.[140] Fathers also play a critical role in ensuring a secure attachment,[141] and the nature of the father-child relationship has been shown to influence children's relationships with others in their later life.[142]

Fourth, without active intervention, the processes inherent in nurturing family relationships may span generations. The nature of family relationships experienced in childhood is often mirrored in the ones established as an adult.[143] A study that spanned four generations, for example, found repeated patterns linking parents' unstable personalities, conflicted marriages, and hostile parenting to children's behavior problems across generations. Conversely, in a large, random sample of thirteen-year-old schoolchildren who were followed up in their thirties, the experience of good parenting in early adolescence predicted their own constructive parenting in adulthood. Despite increasing evidence regarding its intergenerational nature, however, it is not inevitable that the patterns of parenting in one generation are repeated in the next.[144]

A positive spousal relationship is a key factor in building resilience not only for parents but also for children.

This leads to the final point: **a positive spousal relationship** is a powerful force of family strength for both parents and their children. Research, for example, has found that

---

139 N. J. Cabrera, B. L. Volling, and R. Barr, "Fathers are parents, too! Widening the lens on parenting for children's development," *Child Development Perspectives*, 12(3) (2018): 152–157.

140 Ibid.

141 M. E. Lamb and C. Lewis, "Father-child relationships," *Handbook of Father Involvement: Multidisciplinary Perspectives*, 2 (2013): 119–135.

142 H. K. Flynn, D. H. Felmlee, X. Shu, and R. D. Conger, "Mothers and Fathers Matter: The Influence of Parental Support, Hostility, and Problem Solving on Adolescent Friendships," *Journal of Family Issues*, 39(8) (2018): 2389–2412.

143 A. Shaffer, K. B. Burt, J. Obradović, J. E. Herbers, and A. S. Masten, "Intergenerational continuity in parenting quality: The mediating role of social competence," *Developmental Psychology*, 45(5) (2009): 1227.

144 R. D. Conger, J. Belsky, and D. M. Capaldi, "The intergenerational transmission of parenting: Closing comments for the special section," *Developmental Psychology*, 45(5) (2009): 1276–1283.

a nurturing and supportive spousal relationship can help break the intergenerational cycle of harsh and rejecting parenting. In a three-generation, twenty-two-year-long study of five hundred early adolescents followed into adulthood, researchers observed parenting and partner behaviors at three points in time.[145] They found that nurturing and supportive behaviors such as partner warmth and positive communication disrupted the continuity of ineffective parenting experienced in childhood. Another study of institutional-reared women found that those who had purposefully chosen a supportive spouse, based on a conscious and well-planned decision, were better adjusted and more effective parents.[146]

The positive effects of spousal relationships are shown not only for the parents themselves but also for their children. For those who experienced a disadvantaged childhood, the stability and security of the married relationship are especially potent. Enhancing the couple's ability to resolve disagreements and solve problems effectively in their relationship as partners can produce substantial benefits in terms of enhanced marital interactions, more effective parenting strategies, and better outcomes for their offspring, perhaps even into the next generation.

The centrality of the spousal relationship resonates with the Jewish perspective. In *Shir Hashirim* (Song of Songs), the relationship between a husband and wife is a metaphor for the relationship between God and the Jewish People, which highlights the holiness of the marital union. This is exemplified in Rabbi Akiva's statement: "All the writings are holy, but the Song of Songs is the Holy of Holies."[147] Rabbi Akiva expounds: "If a man (*ish*) and woman (*ishah*) merit reward through a faithful marriage, the Divine Presence rests between them. The words *ish* and *ishah* are almost identical; the difference between them is the

---

145   Ibid.
146   D. Quinton and M. Rutter, "Parenting Behavior of mothers raised in care" in *Longitudinal Studies in Child Psychology and Psychiatry* (London: Wiley, 1985).
147   *Mishnah Yadayim* 3:5.

middle letter *yud* in *ish*, and the final letter *hei* in *ishah*. These two letters can be joined to form the name of God spelled *Yud-Hei*."[148]

In this sense, the relationship between husband and wife has the potential to be a Holy of Holies: a resting place for the Shechinah. However, this depends on whether the husband and wife are meritorious, with *shalom bayis* (peace in the home). The Hebrew words for man and for woman both contain the word *eish* (fire). If the couple is contemptible and God's Presence departs, their relationship will be consumed by fire. Adjacent to the word *eish* is the Divine name that is numerically equivalent to fifteen, representing the fifteen rungs upon which the Divine bounty descends from the celestial realms to the earth.[149] This teaches us that our earthly actions in marriage are connected to the higher spiritual world, affecting all aspects of life, both physical and spiritual.[150] With this, we are given insight into the extraordinary potential of the spousal relationship to bring holiness into our own homes in all that this entails. Research confirms what our Sages understood already—that the spousal relationship is the cornerstone of the family. Long ago, our Sages imbued this message with spiritual power: marriage represents *the* vehicle through which we can actualize our greatest potential and ensure our transcendence.

RELATIONSHIP EXERCISE

Love is an active expression. Demonstrate affection to your loved ones every single day through both words and actions.

- Communicate love. Tell your loved ones what you love about them and make this extra special and personal. "I love the way you are so happy to see me when I get home." "I was so thrilled to receive the incredible note that you sent me today." "I love how you are always so willing to lend a helping hand."

---

148 *Sotah* 17a.
149 Rabbi Avraham Yitzchak HaLevi Kilav, Sivan 5764, "Husband and Wife," https://www.yeshiva.co/midrash/2346.
150 Ibid.

- Be affectionate. We all need hugs. When the time is right, give your loved one a twenty-second hug, which research suggests is enough time to release oxytocin, which can lower blood pressure and reduce the stress hormone norepinephrine.[151]
- Act kind. Consider what you can do to make the lives of your loved ones better. This might mean emptying the dishwasher without being asked or baking their favorite cookies.
- Use effective praise. Be specific, make praise authentic, and focus on the person. Instead of "Nice dress," remark, "That blue dress really brings out the color of your beautiful eyes."
- Smile. Whatever you do, make sure you do it with a loving hand. This helps ensure that your effort will be perceived as affectionate.

Here is a game that will help to build connection and bonding with your family, which children will especially enjoy.

COPYCAT GAME

Gather your family together. Make sure you have a clear space. The basic idea is that one person does something and the others then copy that person. Start with some simple movements and then build up to more complex and crazy ones. Some examples include jumping jacks, cartwheels, ballerina twirls, marching, and making a funny face or a funny noise. Each person takes a turn being the leader. The leader says, "Can you copy me?" to the rest of the group, and then everyone performs their best copycat. What is so great about this game is that it makes everyone tune into and pay attention to one another, one at a time. Games, such as this one, are a great way to feel more connected as a family.

151 K. M. Grewen, B. J. Anderson, S. S. Girdler, and K. C. Light, "Warm partner contact is related to lower cardiovascular reactivity," *Behavioral Medicine*, 29(3) (2003): 123–130.

Family Communication

Communication is considered the bedrock of our relationships, which forms the basis of our interactions and feelings about one another. Communication expresses how we feel about another person and shows whether we respect, care, and value them. Effective communication enables us to understand a person better and enriches our relationship with them. Communication is how we truly connect with each other; it is the vehicle through which all of our social relationships are developed and sustained.

Communication not only involves speaking but also incorporates how we listen, share feelings, empathize, brainstorm, and problem-solve. Communication is conveyed through the tone of our voice and our choice of language, eye contact, facial expressions, hand gestures, and body stance.

Communication, by its very nature (and Latin derivative), involves sharing. We might express our thoughts, "listen" to someone else, and judge their facial expressions and body stance, but this does not constitute real communication. Effective communication between two people is when both assign similar meanings and listen carefully to what is being discussed, and they feel heard and understood.

> How a family communicates with one another is one of the most powerful insights into their resilience.

How a family communicates with one another is one of the most powerful insights into their resilience. Research has outlined key processes of communication that support family resilience, including:[152]

- having clear and consistent communication;
- sharing a range of feelings from happiness to sadness;
- being empathetic to one another and tolerating differences;
- taking responsibility for one's own mistakes and avoiding blaming others;
- enjoying pleasant and humorous conversations;

---

152   F. Walsh, "Family resilience: A framework for clinical practice," *Family Process*, 42(1) (2003): 1–18.

- creative brainstorming together;
- having an atmosphere of mutual respect;
- discussing important family decisions;
- focusing on goals and making plans to achieve them;
- being proactive and preventing future problems.

Communication fosters resilience when it provides a sense of clarity regarding a difficult or challenging situation. Although some families prefer not to discuss precarious situations such as past traumas and recurring illnesses, having family secrets often generates fear, anxiety, and uncertainty. Sharing crucial information, when age-appropriate, encourages a feeling of connection and facilitates family meaning-making. When there is secrecy, this slows recovery and can even possibly lead to estrangement among family members.

Open communication and freedom of emotional expression are also essential for family resilience.[153] When families allow one another to share their emotions freely and without criticism, they feel validated and supported. An atmosphere of open communication is especially important during challenging life events when emotions are heightened. When facing a difficult situation, family members may sometimes be out of sync with one another emotionally. They may withdraw, others may erupt in anger and become controlling, and some may continue to be sorrowful. If emotions are denied their expression and family members feel judged, this can impede healing and result in resentment.[154]

Conflict management and collective decision-making are another important part of family communication.[155] Conflict resolution involves negotiating among different viewpoints and compromising with a sense of mutual respect and reciprocation. This allows each member of the family to express their ideas as well as to listen to one another. Family brainstorming further encourages the development of essential coping skills such as problem-solving and planning. Children develop feelings

---

153   Ibid.
154   Ibid.
155   Ibid.

of perceived control and self-respect when they are empowered to engage in shared decision-making, in a manner that is age appropriate. When families work together to solve a problem, they are better able to shift from being reactive to taking a proactive stance, facing challenges head on now and in the future.[156]

How we respond to positive news from our loved ones also influences their well-being, as well as our relationship with them. Capitalization is the idea that telling others about positive events in our life generates benefits, over and above the positive affect associated with the event itself.[157] Capitalization has been linked to increased positive emotions, life satisfaction, and self-esteem and lower feelings of loneliness.[158] Capitalization can also improve our relationship with the responder (the person with whom we are sharing our good news). Relationship benefits associated with capitalization include greater intimacy, closeness, satisfaction, trust, commitment, and stability.[159]

Whether we experience a surplus of positive emotions or not depends on how the responder reacts to our good news. Research shows that there are four ways of responding to someone who is sharing a positive event.[160]

- **Active Constructive** is when the responder shows positive emotions like interest and pride and expresses excitement and enthusiasm about the event. They ask questions and seek additional details. They also elaborate on the meaning of the event for the person.
- **Passive Constructive** is when the person disclosing the event perceives a positive attitude, but the responder does not say much or is silent. This usually involves a pleasant but quick

---

156   Ibid.
157   C. A. Langston, "Capitalizing on and coping with daily-life events: Expressive responses to positive events," *Journal of Personality and Social Psychology*, 67(6) (1994): 1112.
158   S. L. Gable and H. T. Reis, "Good news! Capitalizing on positive events in an interpersonal context," in *Advances in Experimental Social Psychology* (Academic Press, 2010), vol. 42, pp. 195–257.
159   Ibid.
160   Ibid.

exchange. The responder does not ask questions about the event or elaborate on its meaningfulness for the person.

- **Passive Destructive** is when the event is minimally acknowledged by the responder. The responder might convey little or no interest in the event or its implications. The responder might also immediately change the subject to discuss something different or direct the conversation to something about him or her.
- **Active Destructive** is when the responder is attentive and involved, but the feedback is negative. The responder might point out the negative implications of the event, reframe the event as less favorable, and minimize the event's significance.

Here is an example. Let's say someone tells their spouse that they have just received an award for their community involvement. An active constructive response might be: "That's amazing. I'm so happy that the committee recognizes the hard work you have put into planning the community picnic. This is a big step for you, especially as you might run for the community board." A passive constructive response might be: "That's nice. Congratulations." A passive destructive response might be: "What would you like to do tomorrow? You will never believe what happened to me today." An active destructive response might be: "Oh no, that means that they are going to ask you to plan the picnic every year now." As we might expect, capitalizers experience more positive effects from sharing their good news when they perceive that the response is active constructive rather than passive and/or destructive.[161]

The power of communication, through both our speech as well as our silence, is a central tenet of Judaism. Our Sages teach us about effective communication. They advise about what we should and should not discuss. We are given strict instructions regarding what to avoid, which includes gossiping and other hurtful speech. "Guard your tongue from evil, and your lips from speaking deceit."[162] We are also instructed on what is permissible speech: "Two who sit and have words of Torah

---

161 Ibid.
162 *Tehillim* 34.

between them, the Divine Presence is between them..."[163] These statements convey the importance of our words and their impact on one another. Words have the power to uplift as well as to destroy. With this in mind, our communication should reflect the central messages of the Torah, which means that they should focus on goodness, as an expression of Godliness.

We are also instructed about how we should talk to one another. As Shlomo HaMelech has written: "The words of the wise are heard when spoken with gentleness."[164] In Talmudic tradition, we learn that the House of Hillel was privileged to have the halachah established in accordance with their opinion.[165] The reason is that they were agreeable and forbearing, showed restraint when offended, and taught both their own perspective as well as that of the House of Shammai.[166] In fact, when they formulated their teaching and cited a dispute, they gave precedence to the perspective of the House of Shammai before their own.[167] This emphasizes that we must communicate in a way that shows empathy and fosters compromise. Again, the message here is that communication should be used to connect and build unity among us and with God, not to impart division nor inspire strife.

Our Sages also instruct us on when we should talk. There is an appropriate time and place to express our thoughts and feelings. There are also times when silence is warranted or even necessary. According to the Talmud: "A word is worth one coin; silence is worth two."[168] The death of the sons of Aharon, Nadav and Avihu, is a good case in point. The Torah teaches us that Nadav and Avihu each brought a "strange fire" to the Tabernacle which they were either not commanded to bring or commanded *not* to bring, depending on the interpretation.[169] As a

---

163 *Pirkei Avos* 3:2.
164 *Koheles* 9:17.
165 *Eruvin* 13b.
166 Ibid.
167 Ibid.
168 *Megillah* 18a.
169 *Vayikra* 10:1.

result, they were consumed by fire.[170] We are told that they acted alone without communicating with Moshe or Aharon and without consulting each other.[171] Thus, their communication, or lack thereof, played a pivotal role in their death.

In the aftermath, Moshe approached Aharon to comfort him and told him: "This is what the Lord said, 'Through those near to Me, I show Myself Holy and gain glory through all the people.'"[172] In response, Aharon was silent. Moshe further reveals to Aharon that his sons died to sanctify God and that their deaths in the Tabernacle intensified "its awe in the eyes of the people."[173] We are told that: "When Aharon saw how exalted were his sons in the eyes the Lord, he kept his peace and was rewarded for doing so."[174] In the wake of tragedy, Aharon chose to be silent, perhaps resisting what might be considered the more likely response of expressing anger and blaming others; his restraint succeeded in bringing unity among the nation and elevating himself in the process.

As Shlomo HaMelech states: there is a "time to be silent and a time to speak."[175] When words bring healing, comfort, and happiness; encourage empathy, understanding, and unity; and promote conflict resolution, problem-solving, and planning, they are worthy of expression. At the same time, words can be destructive; they can create obstacles, trigger resentment, and breed division. While it can be challenging not to speak up, set the record straight, or blame someone or something else for our pain, restraint is often the higher road that leads us to a more elevated place. In order to maximize understanding, collaboration, and connection within our families, we must carefully consider the nature of our communication in any given situation.

---

170 Ibid., 10:2.
171 *Sifra, Shemini* 2:32.
172 *Vayikra* 10:3.
173 *Sifra, Shemini* 2:32.
174 Ibid.
175 *Koheles* 3:7.

COMMUNICATION EXERCISE

This exercise draws on the work of Shelly Gable and her colleagues, which shows that there are different styles of responding to someone who is sharing a positive event.[176] We make the most of someone sharing their good news when we respond in a way that is active and constructive. Now, consider how you could change your response to better capitalize on the benefits of someone relating their good news.

1. Remember a recent experience when someone shared a positive event.
2. Write out how you could respond in a way that is passive constructive and passive destructive.
3. Write out how you respond in a way that is active destructive.
4. Now, write out how you could respond in a way that is active constructive.

Use the template below to help you with this exercise.

	Active	Passive
Constructive	My family usually reacts to my good news with enthusiasm and excitement.	My family says little, but I know they are happy and excited for me.
Destructive	My family usually points out the potential problems or downsides of my good news.	My family usually does not say much, and I get the impression that they do not care or are not happy for me.

There are many family games that can promote effective communication. Here is an exercise for adults and older children/teens from the team at MindTools.[177] This exercise will help your family enhance their

---

176   S. L. Gable, H. T. Reis, E. A. Impett, and E. R. Asher, "What do you do when things go right? The intrapersonal and interpersonal benefits of sharing positive events," *Journal of Personality and Social Psychology*, 87(2) (2004): 228.

177   https://www.mindtools.com/pages/article/team-building-communication.htm.

empathy, consider one another's perspectives, and teach important communication and negotiation skills.

CARD PIECES

Here's how the game works:

1. Take one pack of regular playing cards. Cut each card in half diagonally, then diagonally in half again, so you have four triangular pieces for each card.
2. Divide everyone into teams of three or four people. Three teams are ideal but two will also work.
3. Mix the pieces and place equal numbers of the pieces into as many piles as you have teams.
4. Give each team a pile of the card pieces.
5. Each team has three minutes to sort its pieces, examine which ones are needed to make complete cards, and brainstorm on a bargaining strategy.
6. After three minutes, teams barter with one another for pieces. People can barter on their own or with their team. Teams have a total of eight minutes to barter.
7. When the time is up, count each team's completed cards. The team with the most cards wins the round.

After the game, these questions can be used as a discussion:

- How did your team work together to devise a bartering strategy?

- What negotiation strategies worked best? What strategies did not work? Why do you think this was the case?
- What might have you done better next time?
- What skills are needed to be successful in this game?

Here is another fun game, which is especially enjoyable for children.

CIRCLE TIME

Sit on the floor or on chairs in a circle facing one another. One person begins with a question and everyone goes around the circle, taking turns to answer the question. Questions might include: "What animal would you choose to be?" "If you could go anywhere in the world, where would you go?" "What's one thing you're grateful for?" or "What would be the worst thing to eat in the whole world?" When that question is done, the next person gets to ask a question and everyone has to answer. At the Shabbos table, family members can also take turns explaining when during the week they experienced *hashgachah pratis* (Divine Providence). This exercise encourages everyone to stop and listen to one another, and allows each person to be the center of attention.

Family Management and Organization

Families need effective management to function. A functioning household requires rules and a clear structure, as well as a schedule in place to facilitate the organization of daily activities. At the same time, some flexibility is important to respond to the inevitable changes and complexities of family life.

For families with young children, much about parenting involves organization. Parents set their children's mealtimes, bath times, and bedtimes. They arrange how their children are getting to and from school and what they are doing after school. They determine household rules about children's exposure to videogames and the Internet, as well as their use of cell phones and other electronic devices.

Parents' management styles can range from relatively inflexible to more laissez-faire and from clear to vague. If clear, parents establish well-defined rules and regulations about what is or is not acceptable. If vague, parents' decision-making often takes the form of unstated indecision—or even indifference.

Research generally agrees that structured parenting, in the context of warmth and support, is the most beneficial environment for families. This involves:

- setting clear, consistent rules;
- using effective but noncoercive limit-setting;
- having nonintrusive boundaries;
- establishing routines, including having meals, doing chores, or sharing activities;
- being open to change and reorganization, when necessary.

A well-managed and organized family setting contributes to a sense of stability and security and forms the basis for learning self-regulation and self-care.[178] When parents set and adhere to regular mealtimes, bedtimes, and media consumption, there are reductions in rates of obesity and substance use, and improved mental and physical health for their children.[179]

During stressful times, a consistent and structured family life is especially important.[180] When a traumatic experience occurs, it inevitably

---

178   H. I. McCubbin and M. A. McCubbin, "Typologies of resilient families: Emerging roles of social class and ethnicity," *Family Relations* (1988): 247–254.

179   F. Traub and R. Boynton-Jarrett, "Modifiable resilience factors to childhood adversity for clinical pediatric practice," *Pediatrics*, 139(5) (2017): e20162569.

180   K. Black and M. Lobo, "A conceptual review of family resilience factors," *Journal of Family Nursing*, 14(1) (2008): 33–55.

brings changes to our life as we know it and acts as a reminder that much of life is uncontrollable. For children who have yet to develop the necessary coping strategies to deal with such an event, the maintenance of routines and consistency of rules provide a sense of normalcy. This reassures children that there are aspects of life that are reliable and dependable. Structure and consistency further exert their positive effects by reinforcing children's personal strengths such as their perceived control and self-regulation, while family routines, such as eating dinner together, provide a context where positive interactions can occur.

> Routines are important for children and adults alike, especially in the wake of trauma.

While most research has examined the importance of management and organization for children, there is growing awareness that routines are also important for adults, especially in the wake of trauma. When experiencing tragedy, the maintenance of one's usual routine helps get our life back on track and aids recovery.[181] For those recovering from a mental health illness such as depression, post-traumatic stress disorder, or substance abuse, the establishment of a healthy routine is considered essential in managing time and planning for better choices.[182] Unstructured time may lead to an increased risk of engaging in unhealthy behaviors. Healthy routines structured around eating, sleeping, and exercising are particularly important to make life more manageable.

While structure and organization are important, flexibility is also a core process in family resilience.[183] When dealing with traumatic and difficult situations, families require some amount of reorganization and adaptation. Families often need to reconstruct a new sense of normalcy when facing life-changing circumstances. Family resilience is fostered when existing routines are recalibrated, and patterns of interaction are reorganized to maximize continuity and minimize disruption.

---

181   https://www.nhs.uk/oneyou/every-mind-matters/trauma/.

182   http://www.mentalhealthcenter.org/boring-self-care-importance-routines/.

183   F. Walsh, "Traumatic loss and major disasters: Strengthening family and community resilience," *Family process*, 46(2) (2007): 207–227.

Judaism embodies a natural framework for managing and maintaining routines. There are numerous daily mitzvos that organize our day, including *Modeh Ani*, morning handwashing, the *Shema*, and the blessing before drinking (and these are just within the first hour upon rising!). Most centrally, our lives revolve around the celebration of Shabbos on a weekly basis. Shabbos offers an oasis of calm in our frantic modern life. It represents a day of rest from the creation of tangible things, focusing instead on the (re)creation and renewal of that which is holy. This includes our relationship with God, as well as our relationships with our family. Shabbos provides us with a concentrated period in which we can build and maintain a warm and positive atmosphere and stable home life. When Shabbos is filled with love, children and adults alike look forward to spending this special time together.

ORGANIZATIONAL EXERCISE

A routine provides families with a structure to function and achieve what needs to be accomplished every day. Having a routine also relieves stress, as there is a clear plan for what needs to be done and when everyone should do it. Here are some ideas for creating and maintaining a family schedule. It is important, however, to ensure that there is some flexibility, as we all need a bit of spontaneity.

- Make a timetable. Break each day into thirty-minute blocks and schedule your family's activities. This provides a greater sense of control over time and a better understanding of what needs to be prioritized. This also helps pinpoint when "me time" or "us time" is available.
- Establish family mealtimes. Eating meals together is an excellent way to reconnect with your family as well as have a sense of structure and stability.
- Set a regular bedtime routine, such as reading a story, having a cuddle, and saying *Shema* together. This teaches children that bedtime involves a routine of relaxing and winding down. This also provides special attention to each and every child at the end of the day, even if it is only for five to ten minutes.

- Make sure the morning has a good start. Mornings can be stressful and rushed, but they do not have to be. Prepare the night before as much as possible, even simple details. Positive morning routines can set everyone's whole day on the right track.
- Schedule regular family meetings. These can focus on your family's upcoming schedule as well as allow everyone to have a voice on how they spend their time. This teaches children important planning skills and provides a time when families can talk about their goals and accomplishments. You might try asking the following questions at these meetings: "What worked well this week? What didn't work well? What should we try to improve in the week ahead?"

Family Meaning Systems

Families, like individuals, need to have a sense of meaning to be resilient. Together, families weave a meaning system about what they believe, who they are, and how they approach life. These meaning systems constitute processes of resilience that are embedded in a family. When meaning systems are positive, they enable the family to mobilize strength during times of adversity. Conversely, negative meaning systems can heighten family risk when faced with trauma. Researchers have delineated family meaning systems into family worldviews, family identity, and situational meanings.[184]

In every family, there are assumptions, belief systems and practices, and outlooks that inform and influence how they see view the world. **Family worldviews** shape patterns of family interactions as well as responses to stressful and challenging situations.[185] Family assumptions involve expectations that are understood but most often unspoken. This might include, for example, assumptions about the roles of men and women, the purpose of marriage, and how children should behave. Similarly, families are characterized by shared moral belief systems that

---

184   J. M. Patterson and A. W. Garwick, "Levels of meaning in family stress theory," *Family Process*, 33(3) (1994): 287–304.

185   C. S. Henry, A. Sheffield Morris, and A. W. Harrist, "Family resilience: Moving into the third wave," *Family Relations*, 64(1) (2015): 22–43.

inform practices and behavior. The obvious example is religion, but this might also include political or other ideologies. These family outlooks frame how life events are viewed within the greater context.

Resilient families have an optimistic outlook on life. They are future-orientated and full of hope, striving to surmount obstacles and realize aspirations. They accept what cannot be changed and focus on what can. They acknowledge their strengths, which encourage feelings of courage, pride, and confidence, along with a can-do attitude.[186] They also have a strong positive moral belief system, which provides a sense of meaning and purpose beyond themselves, their families, and their own challenges. In other words, resilience-building worldviews in the family are similar to those found in a resilient individual.

> Resilient families have an optimistic outlook on life; they are future-orientated and hopeful; they accept what cannot be changed and focus on what can.

What is also important are those assumptions that adults may adhere to without reflection and those that children may infer from their parents' communication and behavior. Someone might, for example, hold unrealistic expectations about their spouse that lead to resentment and unhappiness in marriage when their spouse fails to live up to these unattainable standards. It is also possible that parents may hold high expectations about the nature of achievement, which then translates into high-anxiety children. Children may also surmise assumptions about their own self-worth when parents do not listen to their concerns and engage in absentminded parenting, such as looking at their cell phones during family activities. Although challenging, it is critical to identify negative family assumptions that are conveyed through speech and actions and focus on recrafting more constructive assumptions that foster resilience.

186 F. Walsh, "Family resilience: A framework for clinical practice," *Family Process*, 42(1) (2003): 1–18.

FAMILY WORLDVIEW EXERCISE

Create a family manifesto that highlights your family's shared beliefs, values, strengths, and ways of interacting. This activity is a fun way to encourage family connection and bonding.

1. Gather your family together and each person writes down five to ten answers to the following questions:

   - What does our family believe?
   - What is important to our family?
   - How do we believe we should treat one another?
   - How do we believe we should treat others?
   - How do we respond when faced with a challenge?
   - What are the top strengths of our family?

2. Discuss each person's answers and together choose ten to twenty-five ideas that describe your family best.

3. Create your manifesto in a creative way and then display it in a prominent place.

4. Review your manifesto on a regular basis to make changes and add new ideas, as necessary.

If someone was asked to describe their identity, they would most likely choose their attributes, roles, or characteristics that they most identify with and are most salient in their perception of themselves. For example, they might describe themselves as a teacher, vegetarian, and runner. Like individuals, families also have an identity. When there is a **cohesive family identity**, there is a sense of belonging, a feeling of being part of a team. A family identity also helps to highlight shared values and interests. As a family, you might be nature lovers, book readers, and tennis players. A family identity represents guiding ideas and ways of interacting. As a family, you might "be there for each other through thick and thin." A strong family iden-

A strong family identity offers a sense of security and stability, along with practical and emotional support, which builds resilience.

tity offers a sense of security and stability, along with practical and emotional support, which builds resilience.[187]

A divisive family identity, on the other hand, highlights individual differences and creates separation. In these types of families, individual family members are given different labels that stick like glue and often create a self-fulfilling prophecy. One person might be the "smart one," another might be the "troublemaker," and so forth. These rifts often grow over time, leading to estranged and even sometimes contentious relationships as siblings drift apart in adulthood and create their own families.

On Friday night, Jewish parents give each of their children a blessing. The first part of the blessing for daughters begins, "May God make you like Sarah, Rivkah, Rachel, and Leah," and the first part for sons begins, "May God make you like Ephraim and Menasheh." Why does the blessing for daughters focus on the Matriarchs, while the blessing for the sons focuses on Yosef's sons rather than the Patriarchs, Avraham, Yitzchak, and Yaakov?

There are several reasons given:

- One is that Ephraim and Menasheh grew up in a non-Jewish environment, Egypt. Yet, they were God-fearing, following in the footsteps of their forefathers.
- Another reason is that Ephraim and Menasheh represent brotherly love. When Yaakov blessed his grandchildren, he crossed his hands, giving preference to the younger son over the older one. Nevertheless, there was no jealousy between the brothers.
- Ephraim and Menasheh represent the first pair of brothers who had no strife between them, unlike Kayin and Hevel, Yitzchak and Yishmael, Yaakov and Eisav, and Yosef and his brothers. This is the first instance in the Torah of a strong family identity, and this is also the period when Yosef and his brothers made peace. A strong sense of family identity enabled our ancestors to

---

187 C. S. Henry, A. Sheffield Morris, and A. W. Harrist, "Family resilience: Moving into the third wave," *Family Relations*, 64(1) (2015): 22–43.

become united in their purpose, which marks the beginning of the Jewish nation.

In the present day, mothers and fathers bless that there will be love and peace among their children to ensure family and spiritual continuity.

FAMILY IDENTITY EXERCISE

There is a saying that goes: "Families that play together stay together." Sharing happy and fun times as a family is an essential part of building a positive shared identity. Here are some tips for playing together as a family.

- Make Shabbos the best day. We are so blessed to have one day a week when we can be together as a family. Make an effort to play with your children on Shabbos, which can include imaginative play, reading books together, and playing games. Playing games is a great way for children to feel a part of a team and learn to win and lose in a friendly, nonthreatening way.

- Take advantage of those times when you can talk spontaneously with your children. Running errands and going to and from after-school activities offer opportunities to casually chat with your children about their thoughts and activities.

- Make family chores fun. We all need to empty the dishwasher, fold the laundry, and peel vegetables. If possible, try to make some of these chores a family activity, where everyone pitches in, as a team.

- Make family memories unforgettable. When you go on a fun outing or trip together, take pictures and make an album. After the trip, remind your spouse and children of the fun times you shared together. These shared, positive memories are important sources of bonding for families.

- Emphasize the family unit. Whenever possible, engage in activities that bring the family closer. This might include going bowling as a team or camping together, where everyone has an important role to contribute.

- Honor family traditions. All families have traditions, whether this means baking challah together, going out for ice cream on Rosh Chodesh, or celebrating birthdays with a bang.

Another aspect of family meaning systems is **situational meanings**, which refers to how a family defines and gives meaning to a stressful situation or traumatic event. For any demanding circumstance, families construct a shared understanding about what the event signifies for their family and whether their family has the capability to cope effectively with it.[188] These situational meanings influence how a family responds to challenging episodes.

In terms of different responses to a stressful event, one family might disassociate and disengage from any upheaval, almost like a turtle hiding in its shell. Another might go full steam ahead with a solution, without taking much time for reflection. Another response is to be emotive, maximizing the nature of the problem until everyone feels even more anxious and distressed.

In contrast to these possibilities, resilient families construct a shared meaning about the event and discuss available coping strategies and resources to deal with the issue at hand.[189] A family's capability to manage challenges is considered a keystone of building resilience.[190] Being successful in coping with one situation creates the foundation for a stronger belief system in the family, leading to further resilience when other stressful situations arise in the future.[191]

> A family's capability to manage challenges is a keystone of building resilience.

Miriam and her parents, Amram and Yocheved, provide a good example of how a family can work together to change the meaning of a traumatic event. When Pharaoh ordered that all the Jewish baby boys

188   J. M. Patterson, "Integrating family resilience and family stress theory," *Journal of Marriage and Family*, 64(2) (2002): 349–360.
189   Ibid.
190   Ibid.
191   Ibid.

be thrown into the Nile River, Amram and Yocheved decided to separate as they already had one boy and one girl. As Amram was the leader of the Jewish People during the slavery in Egypt, this prompted all of the other couples to separate to prevent this tragedy as well. Young Miriam, who was a prophetess, explained to her father, "Your decree is harsher than that of Pharaoh! He only decreed against the males, but you have decreed against both the males and the females. It is doubtful whether the decree of the wicked Pharaoh will come to pass, but you are righteous, and so your decree will be fulfilled."[192] Furthermore, since all of the other couples followed their example, no one would have children, which would mean the end of the Jewish nation. Amram saw the wisdom in his daughter's words and he and Yocheved remarried. Following Amram's lead, all the other couples did the same. Miriam prophesized that they would have a son who would save the Jewish nation. The following year, Moshe was born, thus ensuring that the meaning of this traumatic event was transformed into a redemptive one.

SITUATIONAL MEANING EXERCISE

When faced with a stressful family event, consider following these steps to create more manageable expectations regarding its difficulty as well as to enhance your family's ability to cope with the situation.

1. Stop catastrophic thinking in its tracks. Catastrophic thinking is when we ruminate about irrational, worst-case scenarios, which can increase stress, induce anxiety, and discourage problem-solving.

> We all tend to engage in catastrophic thinking from time to time. However, it is important not to let it get out of control and lead to an anxiety spiral, where one negative thought triggers an avalanche of related anxieties. Some examples of spiraling catastrophic thinking include:

192 *Shemos Rabbah* 1.

- "If I fail this exam tomorrow, I might not get into college. Then, I'll be a complete failure and my life will be ruined."
- "If this date doesn't work out, my son/daughter might never meet anyone else who is suitable. They might remain single for the rest of their life."
- "If my spouse has this medical procedure, it could be unsuccessful. They might continue to be unwell and never recover."

To minimize catastrophic thinking, follow these three steps adapted from Seligman and his colleagues:[193]

- First, recognize when your family engages in catastrophic thinking in response to a stressful event and identify what leads to it. For example: Does your family have high expectations in one area, which might prompt insecurities of possible failure? Has something negative happened in the past to your family that fuels fear of something similar happening again?
- Second, rather than focusing on the worst-case scenario, identify the best-case scenario with your family. What is the most ideal outcome of the situation?
- Third, identify the most likely scenario with your family. What is the most probable outcome of the situation?

2. Once your family has identified the most likely outcome to a challenging situation, brainstorm for possible solutions. Here are some tips for successful brainstorming:
   - Accept any and all ideas.
   - Write down all suggestions.
   - Take turns.
   - Wait until everyone has verbalized their ideas before discussing them.

---

193 K. J. Reivich, M. E. Seligman, and S. McBride, "Master resilience training in the US Army," *American Psychologist*, 66(1) (2011): 25–34.

3. After your family has pinpointed a number of possible solutions, choose one. Here is how your family might go about selecting one.

   - First, cross off impossible ideas.
   - Second, write down advantages of the solutions remaining on the list.
   - Third, write down their disadvantages.
   - Last, rank the solutions and choose the highest-ranking one.

4. Now that your family has identified a solution, put it into action. Here are a few suggestions about how you might involve everyone in carrying it out.

   - First, give everyone a role in enacting the solution.
   - Then, decide who will do what and when.
   - Finally, discuss how you will evaluate whether your solution has been successful and, if it is not, what might be an alternative choice to try next.

SUPPORT SYSTEMS

> "Some people think that the environment exerts a significant influence only on children or the weak-minded. This is not true. The environment has important effects even on the greatest."[194]
>
> Rabbi Dessler

As individuals and families, we are embedded in a larger social system and influenced by societal norms, values, laws, and meanings, as well as opportunities and restrictions that exist in the physical environment. These social systems include our friends, communities, and the wider world. These undoubtedly play a role in fostering our resilience, as they represent an avenue of support outside of the family and provide us

---

194   E. E. Dessler, *Strive for the Truth! Part 2*, trans. A. Carmell (Jerusalem: Feldheim, 1978), p. 167.

with resources that can enhance our capacity to build resilience. These resources can be communal, such as identification with a larger group, and practical, such as access to vital services. The most essential of these for boosting resilience include:

- **Friendships**: Do you have friends who are loyal and supportive? Can you rely on your friends in times of trouble? Do you have positive friendships with people who uplift, encourage, and inspire you?
- **Community**: Are there people in your community whom you spend time with? Do you volunteer and help others in your community? Are you able to ask people in your community for help when needed?
- **Nature**: Do you live near nature? Do you spend time in natural surroundings on a regular basis? Do you often stop to appreciate the beautiful world that God has given us?

Friendships

As the saying goes, we cannot choose our family, but we can choose our friends. This thought is empowering. We have the capacity to surround ourselves with those people who will imbue us with resilience and inspire us to become better people.

Why are our friends so important? First, supportive relationships make a significant difference to our physical health and longevity. For example, an investigation examining the average of 148 studies comprised of over 308,000 participants found that having stronger social relationships was related to about a 50% lower risk of death.[195] Some reasons that supportive relationships may influence our health include (1) acting as a buffer from stressful circumstances, (2) encouraging us to have healthy habits, and (3) providing us with practical support when needed.

> We cannot choose our family, but we can choose our friends.

---

195 J. Holt-Lunstad, T. B. Smith, J. B. Layton, "Social relationships and mortality risk: a meta-analytic review," *PLoS Medicine* 7 (2010): 1–20.

Our friendships are also important for our mental health, happiness, and satisfaction with life. Rather than the number of friends (including "online" friends), what seems to be most essential is the nature of our friendships. Having a positive and supportive relationship with a close friend boosts our well-being.[196] A positive friend is characterized as trustworthy, trusting of others, honest, dependable, loyal, empathic, a good listener, nonjudgmental, supportive in both good and bad times, self-confident, humorous, and fun to be around.[197] Positive friends praise our successes and offer encouragement after our failures, share our interests, and believe in similar values and moral codes as we do.[198]

The effects of a positive friendship are long-lasting. Adults who report having a positive relationship (in terms of their encouragement and support) with their best friend reported better health and self-esteem more than ten years later compared to adults who reported having a conflictual relationship with their best friend.[199] The influence of our friendships in childhood and adolescence also extends to adulthood. For example, one study following 169 participants from the age of 15 to 25 found that close friendships in adolescence predicted an increase in self-worth and a decrease in anxiety and depressive symptoms in adulthood.[200]

But what if those good friendships are with people who engage in unhealthy behaviors and experience social and psychological problems? Do good friendships with these kinds of friends have a positive or negative influence on us? Research seems to show that they have a negative

---

196 T. C. Antonucci, "Social relations: An examination of social networks, social support, and sense of control," in J. E. Birren and K. W. Schaie, eds., *Handbook of the Psychology of Aging* (San Diego, CA: Academic Press, 2001), pp. 427–453.

197 https://www.psychologytoday.com/gb/blog/lifetime-connections/201503/the-13-essential-traits-good-friends.

198 R. G. Adams, R. Blieszner, and B. De Vries, "Definitions of friendship in the third age: Age, gender, and study location effects," *Journal of Aging Studies*, 14(1) (2000): 117–133.

199 H. R. Fuller-Iglesias, N. J. Webster, and T. C. Antonucci, "Adult family relationships in the context of friendship," *Research in Human Development*, 10(2) (2013): 184–203.

200 R. K. Narr, J. P. Allen, J. S. Tan, and E. L. Loeb, "Close friendship strength and broader peer group desirability as differential predictors of adult mental health," *Child Development*, 90(1) (2019): 298–313.

influence, especially on children and teens.[201] When children spend more time with friends who engage in rebellious activities like drinking alcohol, stealing, and lying, they are at greater risk for engaging in these types of activities themselves and having academic problems, even if the nature of their friendships is a supportive one.[202]

As we get older, we tend to be more careful about choosing our friends, but adult friendships can still be characterized by negative relational and behavioral patterns, which take their toll on our physical and mental health.[203] As adults, when we have friends who drink alcohol, for example, we are more likely to drink alcohol as well.[204] In a study that spanned over forty years, two researchers found that one's social networks, which included their friends, family, and neighbors, influenced their weight and smoking habits, and even their happiness.[205] Those whose social networks were obese, smoked cigarettes, and unhappy were also more likely to be obese, smoke cigarettes, and unhappy themselves in the future. This is because, as social creatures, we are greatly influenced by others around us, including our friends and family. We tend to become similar to those with whom we associate and those who surround us, and this similarity polarizes over time. In other words, health and happiness are a social phenomenon. If we want to live a positive life, we should surround ourselves with positive people.

In terms of resilience, studies suggest that friendships are even more significant in times of suffering. In adulthood, for example, research

> If we want to live a positive life, we should surround ourselves with positive people.

201   T. J. Berndt, "Friendship quality and social development," *Current Directions in Psychological Science*, 11(1) (2002): 7–10.

202   J. G. Dryfoos, *Adolescents at Risk* (New York: Oxford University Press, 1990).

203   C. L. Bagwell, S. E. Bender, C. L. Andreassi, T. L. Kinoshita, S. A. Montarello, and J. G. Muller, "Friendship quality and perceived relationship changes predict psychosocial adjustment in early adulthood," *Journal of Social and Personal Relationships*, 22(2) (2005): 235–254.

204   C. D. Mohr, S. Averna, D. A. Kenny, and F. K. Del Boca, "Getting by (or getting high) with a little help from my friends: an examination of adult alcoholics' friendships," *Journal of Studies on Alcohol*, 62(5) (2001): 637–645.

205   N. Christakis and J. Fowler, *Connected: The Surprising Power of Our Social Networks and How They Shape Our Lives* (Little, Brown and Company, 2011).

shows that having supportive friends reduces psychological distress for people affected by cancer[206] and helps those who experienced childhood maltreatment be more resilient as adults.[207] The importance of friends in fostering resilience is especially crucial for children experiencing hardship, as they usually do not have many other avenues of support. For maltreated children, for instance, high-quality friendships provide opportunities to learn and practice social skills that are often absent in their own family setting.[208] Academically supportive friends also encourage the school achievement of children living in disadvantaged circumstances.[209]

Our Jewish tradition emphasizes the importance of having good friends. It is said that: "Two are better than one because they have a good reward for their labor. For if they fall, the one will lift up his fellow; but woe to him that is alone when he falls, for he has not another to help him up."[210] In our ancient texts, perhaps the greatest of friendships is that of David and Yehonasan. Yehonasan, the eldest son of Shaul HaMelech (who despised David) and the crown prince, had a deep and loyal friendship with David. We are told that "Yehonasan's soul had become attached to David's soul, and Yehonasan loved him as himself."[211] Although David was a threat to his place in line to the crown, Yehonasan protected David from his father's attempts to have him killed.

In Judaism, the significance of friends extends beyond love and loyalty. The Talmud advises on the importance of selecting friends who improve our learning: "Iron sharpens iron, so a man sharpens the

---

206   I. Hasson-Ohayon, G. Goldzweig, M. Braun, and D. Galinsky, "Women with advanced breast cancer and their spouses: diversity of support and psychological distress," *Psycho-oncology*, 19(11) (2010): 1195–1204.

207   A. Powers, K. J. Ressler, and R. G. Bradley, "The protective role of friendship on the effects of childhood abuse and depression," *Depression and Anxiety*, 26(1) (2009): 46–53.

208   K. E. Bolger and C. J. Patterson, "Sequelae of child maltreatment: Vulnerability and resilience," *Resilience and Vulnerability: Adaptation in the context of childhood adversities* (2003): 156–181.

209   L. M. Gutman, A. J. Sameroff, and J. S. Eccles, "The academic achievement of African American students during early adolescence: An examination of multiple risk, promotive, and protective factors," *American Journal of Community Psychology*, 30(3) (2002): 367–399.

210   *Koheles* 4:9–10.

211   *Shmuel I* 18:1.

countenance of his friend."[212] This verse is further explained to mean that "just as with these iron implements, one sharpens the other when they are rubbed against each other, so too, when Torah scholars study together, they sharpen one another in halachah."[213] Rabbi Chanina also stated: "I have learned much from my teachers and even more from my friends."[214]

Judaism also emphasizes the importance of choosing the right kind of friends. Our Sages state: "It is natural to be influenced in character and conduct by your friends and associates and to follow the local norms of behavior. Therefore, one ought to ensure that your friends are virtuous and that you frequent the company of the wise so that you learn from their deeds. Conversely, you should keep away from the wicked who walk in darkness, so as not to learn from their deeds."[215] This is further emphasized by Shlomo HaMelech's statement: "He who walks with the wise will become wise, while the one who associates with fools will suffer."[216]

These sensible and wise words teach us that our friends influence our thoughts and actions, whether we wish them to or not. With this in mind, we should choose our friends not based on who we are, but rather who we aspire and hope to become.

FRIENDSHIP EXERCISE

High-quality friendships are intimate, close relationships with those who inspire, encourage, support, and motivate us to be productive and healthy individuals. We often do not think about the nature of our friendships; instead we assume that good friends are those people who stick around the longest. It is essential, however, to consider how our friendships are, consciously or not, influencing our feelings and choices.

---

212   *Mishlei* 27:17.
213   *Taanis* 7a.
214   Ibid.
215   *Mishneh Torah, Hilchos De'os,* 6:1.
216   *Mishlei* 13:20.

Reflect on whether you feel better, more empowered, stronger, and happier when you are with your friends. If the answer is yes, then you are doing great. If you sense, however, that some friendships are draining you, making you feel less competent, and leaving you feeling dissatisfied and discontented, then maybe it is time to reconsider the amount of time you spend with those friends. After all, our friendships are an active *choice*. In this sense, if we are choosing to be with people who bring us down, then it's up to us to make a change for the better.

Here are a few questions adapted from those used by psychologists to assess social support.[217] These may be helpful to you in determining whether your friendships are positive and supportive. Consider one specific friend in mind when answering these questions.

- Can you really count on your friend to listen to you when you need to talk?
- Can you really count on your friend to help you out in a crisis situation, even though they would have to go out of their way to do so?
- Can you really count on your friend to be dependable when you need help?
- Can you totally be yourself with your friend?
- Does your friend really appreciate you as a person?
- Can you count on your friend to console you when you are very upset?

Community

What is a community? A community is defined as a collection of individuals and families living in the same place, who share similar beliefs, values, and goals. In Judaism, the *kehillah* (community) provides the essential structure to the Jewish way of life. The Talmud states the following guidelines about what constitutes a Jewish community:

217   I. G. Sarason, H. M. Levine, R. B. Basham, and B. R. Sarason, "Assessing social support: The social support questionnaire," *Journal of Personality and Social Psychology*, 44(1) (1983): 127.

> *A Torah scholar is not permitted to reside in any city that does
> not have these ten things: A court that has the authority to
> flog and punish transgressors, and a charity fund for which
> monies are collected by two people and distributed by three, as
> required by halachah. This leads to a requirement for another
> three people in the city. And a synagogue; and a bathhouse;
> and a public bathroom; a doctor; and a bloodletter; and a scribe
> to write sacred scrolls and necessary documents; and a ritual
> slaughterer; and a teacher of young children.*[218]

In this sense, a Jewish community needs to have the physical, educational, and religious resources to meet the needs of its inhabitants.

In Judaism, being an active part of a community is not simply an option but an obligation. Such that, caring for our community is a mitzvah. This obligation is reflected in the collective response often seen in the wake of a tragedy. When individual tragedy strikes, it affects the entire Jewish community. In my community, a young mother of several children was seriously ill. The community pulled together so that she was not alone even for one minute of the entirety of her time in the hospital. The family's children were taken care of and brought to and from school. There were several sessions of reciting *Tehillim*, with around two hundred people in attendance. This shared response to an individual's tragedy has been witnessed over and over, throughout many communities, highlighting the cohesiveness of the Jewish People in times of need.

Sadly, more and more often, there is community tragedy in the form of violence and natural disaster. In one such tragedy, a horrendous shooting occurred in Jersey City, in 2019, and the victims of the attack were members of the ultra-Orthodox Satmar movement, an insular Chassidic community. Shock and grief were felt and expressed by the

> In Judaism, being an active part of a community is not simply an option but an obligation.

---

218 *Sanhedrin* 17b.

entire Jewish community that stretched from Jersey City to Jerusalem.[219] No matter the denomination, Jewish people shared their condolences and there were hundreds of donations to online fundraisers. Jews from all over the world contacted the bereaved families and some even traveled to Jersey City to express their condolences in person.[220] This demonstrates that despite the differences among us, when tragedy strikes, we are reminded of the historic, religious, and transcendental bonds that unite us as a people.

Research recognizes the inherent potential of community resilience. Similar to individual resilience, community resilience is a process linking the resources of the community to the positive functioning of its inhabitants.[221] These resources might include community-level social support (such as providing community meals), social resources (such as after-school clubs), economic resources (such as charity and food banks), community participation (such as volunteering), information and communication (such as a community newsletter), infrastructure (such as strong community leaders), safety (such as a neighborhood watch and other security features), and recreation (such as parks and walking trails).

Community connectedness is vital for adults and children alike.

Further to the social and physical resources of a community, people's sense of belonging and meaning within the community has implications for their resilience. Community connectedness is vital for adults and children alike, as this provides a safe and constructive way of being part of a larger social environment. A sense of community is a "feeling that members have of belonging and being important to each other, a shared faith that members' needs will be met by the commitment

---

219 https://www.jta.org/2019/12/20/opinion/the-response-to-the-jersey-city-shooting-exemplifies-the-dangers-of-not-taking-hasidic-jews-seriously.

220 https://www.aish.com/jw/s/My-Shiva-Visit-with-the-Ferencz-Sisters-in-Jersey-City.html?mobile=yes.

221 F. H. Norris, S. P. Stevens, B. Pfefferbaum, K. F. Wyche, and R. L. Pfefferbaum, "Community resilience as a metaphor, theory, set of capacities, and strategy for disaster readiness," *American Journal of Community Psychology*, 41(2008): 127–150.

to be together."[222] A feeling of community connectedness has been shown to boost resilience in communities struck by traumatic loss and major disasters[223] as well as those characterized by disadvantages such as poverty.[224]

Communities are made up of their inhabitants, as well as their institutions, such as schools, religious organizations, community and youth centers, and charities. Day-to-day interactions within these institutions build resilience for community members, especially for those who might not be able to access more high-level support. For children, schools have the potential to be an important source of resilience.[225] Teachers play a crucial role as caring adults or mentors for those students who need additional support.[226] School-based interventions can successfully teach children resilience-building skills in the classroom.[227] Effective school-based interventions have been found to boost children's social and problem-solving skills, as well as their school achievement.[228]

A sense of nationhood has long defined the Jewish People. We are *"am Yisrael"* (the Jewish nation), rather than *"das Yisrael"* (the religion of Israel). When we pray, we do so for the whole community of Israel; our Sages formulated almost all of our prayers in plural for this very reason.[229] The Jewish nation as a whole is united in our fortune and fate. We are judged by how we take care of one another, how we speak

222 D. W. McMillian and D. M. Chavis, "Sense of community: a definition and theory," *Journal of Community Psychology*, 14(1) (1986): 6–23.

223 F. Walsh, "Traumatic loss and major disasters: Strengthening family and community resilience," *Family process*, 46(2) (2007): 207–227.

224 J. Wiseman and K. Brasher, "Community wellbeing in an unwell world: Trends, challenges, and possibilities," *Journal of Public Health Policy*, 29(3) (2008): 353–366.

225 M. Rutter, "Psychosocial resilience and protective mechanisms," *American Journal of Orthopsychiatry*, 57(3) (1987): 316–331.

226 L. M. Gutman and C. Midgley, "The role of protective factors in supporting the academic achievement of poor African American students during the middle school transition," *Journal of Youth and Adolescence*, 29(2) (2000): 223–249.

227 L. M. Gutman and I. Schoon, "The impact of non-cognitive skills on outcomes for young people," *Education Endowment Foundation*, 59(22.2) (2013): 2019.

228 L. M. Gutman and I. Schoon, "Preventive interventions for children and adolescents," *European Psychologist*, 20 (2015): 231–241.

229 E. E. Dessler, *Strive for the Truth! Part 2*, trans. A. Carmell (Jerusalem: Feldheim, 1978).

to and about one another, and how we consider one another. "All Israel are responsible for one another."[230] This testifies to the immense power of the *kehillah*.

SOCIAL CONNECTION EXERCISE

Our social connection with others is one of our most powerful protective factors. These social connections need to be created and then maintained. Here are a few thoughts on how to do so.

- Spend time with friends. Make regular dates with friends to meet for coffee and talk. Consider these get-togethers as an essential part of your weekly/monthly schedule.
- Be real. In this time of social media, it can be difficult to be open with people about your own challenges. Doing so breaks down barriers and allows others to see the real you. It also gives people the courage to talk about their own vulnerabilities.
- Tell others when you need support. Giving to and receiving from others creates a connection. Allow others to help you and tell them what you need in order for them to do so effectively.
- Volunteer in your community. It makes us feel good when we help others. It also gives you an opportunity to meet different people in your community and make connections with them.
- Role-model the importance of social connections with your children. Teach children that friends are an important part of our lives and they make us happier. Show them what it means to be a good friend. Take your children on family volunteering days and consider ways that your family can do acts of *chessed* (kindness) in your community.

---

230   Ibid., p. 159.

Nature

> "For now, the winter is past, the rains are over and
> gone. The blossoms have appeared in the land.
> The time of the song-bird has come; the song of
> the turtledove is heard in our land. The green figs
> form on the fig tree, the blossoming vines give off
> fragrance."
>
> Shir Hashirim 2:11–13

The great outdoors is a source of inspiration and revelation. We become awestruck by majestic natural formations, overwhelmed by the immense height of towering ancient trees, and mesmerized by waves crashing against the shore. Nature is a constant reminder of the miracles that God has bestowed on our world. In Judaism, we recognize these astonishing gifts by reciting blessings on mountains, deserts, thunder and lightning, rainbows, exotic animals, beautiful trees, natural bodies of water, astronomical phenomena, earthquakes and fierce winds, and places where miracles occurred. We also recite blessings when we smell pleasant fragrances from flowers and trees. These blessings serve to increase our awareness of God's presence and remind us that these are God's works of creation, which are nothing short of miraculous. According to Rabbi Dessler, nature is a miracle that is concealed by habit.[231]

Instinctively, we know that nature is good for us, both emotionally and physically. The restorative power of nature has long been a discussion point in poems and literature. It has taken science awhile to catch up. Over the past few decades, research has become increasingly interested in the role of nature for our vitality and fitness. Nature has been shown to provide a sense of restored calm and attentiveness and

---

231   E. E. Dessler, *Strive for the Truth! Part 2*, trans. A. Carmell (Jerusalem: Feldheim, 1978), p. 240.

reduce feelings of stress.[232] The benefits of nature are delivered through our sight, sound, smell, taste, and touch.[233] In one study, for example, hospital patients recovering from surgery showed more positive feelings, received fewer negative written comments about their mood and attitude from nurses, and spent less time in the hospital if their room overlooked trees instead of a brick wall.[234] Researchers have also found that natural sounds affect the bodily systems, influencing the resting activity of the brain. In one experiment, participants listened to sounds recorded from natural and artificial environments while their brain activity was measured in an MRI scanner, and their autonomic nervous system activity was monitored via minute changes in their heart rate.[235] When listening to natural compared with artificial sounds, participants experienced more bodily relaxation. Interestingly, the positive effect of natural sounds was most pronounced for those who showed the greatest stress before starting the experiment.

Our exposure to green space (such as trees, gardens, and parks) and blue space (such as lakes, rivers, seas, and other water areas) also seems to play a role in our health and well-being. In large studies of the general population, those who live in neighborhoods with more green space have better perceived health, more physical activity, fewer mental health problems, and lower mortality rates than those who live in areas with less green space.[236] Research also finds that living in areas with more blue space is associated with better physical and mental health, as

232   R. Kaplan and S. Kaplan, *The Experience of Nature: A Psychological Perspective* (Cambridge, England: Cambridge University Press, 1989).

233   L. S. Franco, D. F. Shanahan, and R. A. Fuller, "A review of the benefits of nature experiences: more than meets the eye," *International Journal of Environmental Research and Public Health*, 14(8) (2017): 864–893.

234   R. S. Ulrich, "View through a window may influence recovery from surgery," *Science*, 224(4647) (1984): 420–421.

235   C. D. G. Van Praag, S. N. Garfinkel, O. Sparasci, A. Mees, A. O. Philippides, M. Ware,…and H. D. Critchley, "Mind-wandering and alterations to default mode network connectivity when listening to naturalistic versus artificial sounds," *Scientific Reports*, 7 (2017): 45273.

236   S. Volker and T. Kistemann, "The impact of blue space on human health and well-being—Salutogenetic health effects of inland surface waters: A review," *Int J Hyg Envir Heal*, 214(6) (2011):449–460; A. Lee and R. Maheswaran, "The health benefits of urban green spaces: a review of the evidence," *J Public Health*, 33(2) (2010): 212–222.

well as higher self-esteem.[237] What these studies highlight is the importance of nature for healthy living, both psychologically and physically.

Nature may also bolster resilience for children experiencing multiple hardships. A UK study, for example, found that children experiencing multiple adversities (neighborhood disadvantage, family poverty, and adverse life events) who lived in neighborhoods with more green space had fewer emotional problems than their counterparts who lived in less green neighborhoods.[238]

The Torah informs us that when God was preparing to create man, He used the plural expression, "Let us make man in our image, after our likeness."[239] Given that God is the One who creates humans, what is meant by the use of "us," especially as this is the only time when a plural pronoun is used when referring to Creation during the six days? The traditional explanation is that God used a plural pronoun to teach us that we should consult others, even when One is the single authority. According to *Rashi*, God included the angels in the creation of Adam, as a matter of courtesy. Other commentators, however, have identified another teaching in this plural expression of man's creation.[240] "Since all of Creation was brought into being for the sake of man, God's wisdom ordained that the spiritual essence of every element in the universe should be included in man. It was as if everything collaborated in Adam's creation, by giving him a part of itself, as it were."[241] All of the creatures in the universe are unique unto themselves and unrelated to the others, but humans are different. Humans encompass, and are intertwined with, every part of Creation. When humans rise and fall, so does Creation. In other words, our ascent and descent are not ours

---

237   D. E. Bowler, L. M. Buyung-Ali, T. M. Knight, and A. S. Pullin, "A systematic review of evidence for the added benefits to health of exposure to natural environments," *BMC Public Health*, 10(1) (2010): 456–466.

238   E. Flouri, E. Midouhas, and H. Joshi, "The role of urban neighborhood green space in children's emotional and behavioral resilience," *Journal of Environmental Psychology*, 40 (2014): 179–186.

239   *Bereishis* 1:26.

240   N. Scherman, *The Schottenstein Edition of Perek Shirah: The Song of the Universe* (New York: Mesorah Publications, 2004)

241   Ibid., p. 9.

alone; everything humans do affects the material world. When the Temple stood and Israel was at a high spiritual level, the fruits and vegetables were abundant and flavorful. When the Temple was destroyed, the earth declined with it.[242]

Given this, it is not surprising that spending time in nature is important for our health. It is a Divine connection reminding us of who we are as individuals and as a collective. Judaism is tied to the seasonal variations in the calendar through its daily, monthly, and yearly rituals and observances. On a daily basis, our prayers focus on our appreciation of nature and even change slightly when we are praying during either the winter or summer months. Throughout the Jewish year, our holidays commemorate the different seasons and the lunar cycles. These holidays acknowledge the birth of the trees, springtime, and the harvest months. Together, the practices and observances in Judaism sharpen our spiritual connection with nature, awakening within us feelings of gratitude and contentment and reminding us of our intimate bond with the natural environment.

NATURE EXERCISE

On a regular basis, it is important to reconnect with nature to boost our health and well-being. How much time should we spend in nature to receive its benefits? Research recommends that we spend at least 120 minutes per week outside. A study of nearly 20,000 people in England found that those who spent 120 minutes or more per week in nature (which might include a long hike or a trip to the park) reported better health and well-being than those who reported spending less time outside.[243]

Here are a few ideas on how you might increase the amount of time, as well as the quality of how it is spent, in the great outdoors:

---

242   Ibid.
243   M. P. White, I. Alcock, J. Grellier, B. W. Wheeler, T. Hartig, S. L. Warber, and…L. E. Fleming, "Spending at least 120 minutes a week in nature is associated with good health and wellbeing," *Scientific Reports*, 9(1) (2019): 1–11.

- Walk instead of drive. Take the time to have a leisurely walk and enjoy the scenery.
- Say blessings. We are so blessed to have been given Divine words that remind us of our connection to God's gift of nature. Say these with inspiration and meaning.
- Close your eyes and meditate on being at one with nature. Inhale deeply, reflecting on how you are breathing in oxygen produced by plants, shrubs, and trees. Exhale deeply, reflecting on how plants use your exhalation to produce their own energy.
- Use your senses. When in nature, especially somewhere where there are numerous plants, shrubs, and trees present, smell their leaves and blossoms and gaze at their miraculous beauty and diversity.
- Listen to the calming sounds of nature. Natural sounds including birdsong, the trickle of raindrops, and the rustle of leaves in the wind may contribute to the restorative experience of being in nature.
- Teach your children. Remark on the beauty of our world. Instill respect for nature and teach them that it is our obligation to ensure its health and continuity.

Chapter Five

WHAT IS POST-TRAUMATIC GROWTH?

"I thought I would end my days with my family,
and be as long-lived as the phoenix."

Iyov 29:18

Post-traumatic growth has been referred to as
"flourishing under fire."[1] With this description, one might picture the
phoenix, a mythical bird that lives forever, being rejuvenated every
thousand years, when a fire issues forth and burns it up. All that remains is an egg, from which the phoenix grows and lives again. The
midrash explains that after Chavah ate from the Tree of Knowledge, she
gave its fruit to all of the animals to eat. Only a certain bird, named the

---

1   C. D. Ryff and B. Singer, "Flourishing under fire: Resilience as a prototype of challenged
     thriving," *Flourishing: Positive psychology and the life well-lived* (2003): 15-36.

chol (phoenix), abstained from eating it. Thus, death was decreed upon all animals—except the phoenix.[2]

The phoenix provides a beautiful allegory for the Jewish People and their ability to thrive amid the most devastating circumstances. Similar to the phoenix, the Jewish nation is eternal. Alongside tragedy, there are periods of flourishing in our history. The Jewish People, like the phoenix, rise out of their own ashes and experience rebirth.

HOW CAN SUFFERING PROMOTE POSITIVE GROWTH AND TRANSFORMATION?

In the midst of trauma and tragedy, most of us experience little or no positive growth. When positive changes occur, these usually emerge in the aftermath of adversity. Post-traumatic growth is not a consequence of trauma but rather arises from the struggle to make our suffering meaningful. Those who flourish use their experience of suffering as a vehicle to transcend to a greater reality, transforming their lives and the lives of others in the process.

> Post-traumatic growth is not a consequence of trauma but rather arises from the struggle to make our suffering meaningful.

A central pillar of Judaism is that God has endowed our lives with meaning. Everything we experience has a purpose, including our suffering. In our lives, we are able to withstand great difficulties as long as we can find meaning in our existence. In *Man's Search for Meaning*, Frankl explains how he found meaning—even in his suffering in Auschwitz.[3] Shortly after his arrival, Frankl was stripped of his "mental child"—a manuscript that contained his life's work, which he had hidden in his coat pocket. Realizing that the odds of his survival were "no more than one in twenty-eight," he had what he describes as "perhaps his deepest experience in the concentration camps."

> *I had to undergo and overcome the loss of my mental child. And now it seemed as if nothing and no one would survive me; neither a physical nor a mental child of my own. So, I found*

---

2   *Bereishis Rabbah* 19:5.
3   V. Frankl, *Man's Search for Meaning* (London: Rider, 2004).

myself confronted with the question whether under such cir-
cumstances my life was ultimately void of meaning...Not yet
did I notice that an answer to this question with which I was
wrestling so passionately was already in store for me, and that
soon thereafter this answer would be given to me. This was the
case when I had to surrender my clothes and in turn inherited
the worn-out rags of an inmate who had already been sent
to the gas chamber...Instead of the many pages of my manu-
script, I found in a pocket of the newly acquired coat one single
page torn out of a Hebrew prayer book, containing the most
important Jewish prayer, Shema Yisrael. How should I have
interpreted such a "coincidence" other than as a challenge to
live my thoughts instead of merely putting them on paper?

What is it about the prayer *Shema Yisrael* that inspires meaning in our existence? *Shema Yisrael* sanctifies God as One, addressing our soul's longing to connect with our Creator, aligning us with our true purpose in this world. *Shema Yisrael* reminds us of the Divine Oneness of God: He created the world, He sustains everything, and He is everywhere. Our very existence, everything we are and do, is inseparable from God. What may appear to us as a separation between the physical and spiritual world is merely an illusion. God's Oneness manifests into every aspect of the universe—there is no independent existence other than Him. As partners in Creation, our purpose is to synthesize the physical and spiritual. God created the physical in order for us to complete our mission: to transform and uplift the physical into the spiritual realm. In other words, we use our bodies to perform mitzvos, which elevate the mundane into the holy.

In our society today, however, our identity is often in a state of separation and confusion. Many of us are divorced from our spiritual side, becoming immersed in our material needs. As we become more entangled in our worldly activities, we are lured into believing in cause and effect—assuming we have ultimate control over our own destiny, rather than God. We make mistakes. We wander off the path. We forget our true purpose in this world. This causes spiritual damage to our soul, hindering our relationship with God. However, there are moments when the equilibrium between the body and the soul is re-established.

Tragedy is one of those times. When tragedy strikes, we often detach ourselves from our physical and material desires and concentrate on our spiritual needs instead. The experience of suffering forces us to re-appraise our true purpose in this world and our relationship with our Creator. Through trauma, we learn that we are not in control of the physical world, but instead our existence depends on God. Once we place our trust in God, our physical and spiritual aspects are united. The body acts in accordance with the needs of the soul. It is not coincidental that when faced with certain death, *Shema*—the prayer acknowledging the Oneness of God—is on our lips.

As we move through our lives, we operate on the basis of assumptions and personal theories that allow us to set goals, plan activities, and organize our behavior.[4] These assumptions often include seeing ourselves as having control over events and being relatively invulnerable to harm, viewing life as predictable and orderly, and regarding ourselves as worthy and other people as kind.[5] Many of us are unaware of these fundamental assumptions and the daily struggles of everyday life rarely bring them to light. As creatures of comfort, we resist change and deny minor inconsistencies.

> When tragedy strikes, we often detach ourselves from our physical and material desires, focusing on our spiritual needs instead.

Traumatic circumstances, however, shatter our basic assumptions and personal theories.[6] To grapple with our new reality, we are forced to rebuild and reframe our assumptions about ourself, our life, and our future. This leads to an active contemplation of our thoughts, feelings, and actions. As a result, we gain a greater understanding of ourselves and our capabilities. We reassess our life goals and reset our priorities.

---

4   R. Janoff-Bulman and I. H. Frieze, "A theoretical perspective for understanding reactions to victimization," *Journal of Social Issues*, 39(2) (1983): 1–17.

5   C. M. Parkes, "What becomes of redundant world models? A contribution to the study of adaptation to change," *British Journal of Medical Psychology* (1975).

6   R. Janoff-Bulman, "Rebuilding shattered assumptions after traumatic life events," *Coping: The Psychology of What Works* (1999): 305–323.

We may also develop new ideas about our existential purpose, which influence our beliefs about religion and God.

Similar to the integration of body and soul from the Jewish perspective, research finds the crucial aspect of positive growth through suffering is the combination of emotion and intellect.[7] To experience growth, the explanation for tragedy is neither satisfied with an emotive response nor a rational reflection, but rather the integration of both the affective and intellectual. A traumatic event that promotes positive growth is one that can be seen as a personal lesson, prompting an intellectual and emotional reframing of one's life.

> A traumatic event that promotes positive growth is one that can be seen as a personal lesson, prompting an intellectual and emotional reframing of one's life.

This process is distressing and unpleasant but nevertheless can lead to a more fully developed, satisfying, and meaningful life in the aftermath of tragedy.[8]

WHAT POSITIVE CHANGES MIGHT OCCUR IN THE FACE OF SUFFERING?

The view that one can experience growth and transformation through suffering is ancient and widespread—not only in Judaism but also in other religious, philosophical, and literal traditions.[9] However, the study of positive growth in the face of suffering for scholars and clinicians is relatively recent. Traditional research on resilience focused on **recovery** from stressful and traumatic events but did not recognize that there may actually be **benefits** accrued from suffering.

In one of the earliest studies documenting positive growth in response to trauma, researchers conducted interviews with breast cancer patients to identify those resources that would help them recover from this traumatic and life-threatening illness.[10] In emotional and poignant interviews, the breast cancer survivors reported that rather than

---

7   R. G. Tedeschi and L. Calhoun, "Posttraumatic growth: A new perspective on psychotraumatology," *Psychiatric Times*, 21(4) (2004): 58–60.
8   Ibid.
9   Ibid.
10 Ibid.

getting back to normal, most of their lives had changed—and some for the better.

- Some talked about re-establishing priorities and making time for the activities that were most important to them.
- Others noted how they saw themselves as now being stronger and more self-assured.
- Most found that relationships with family and friends gained significance and they paid more attention to nurturing these relationships.
- Breast cancer survivors who reported such positive changes also tended to feel better about themselves too—reporting better psychological adjustment compared to their counterparts who did not report post-traumatic growth.

Since that time, numerous studies have documented the possible benefits that may occur in response to struggling with traumatic situations. A review of this research finds that these positive changes tend to fall into one of three broad categories:

- Personal changes
- Improved relationships with others
- Philosophies of life

This evidence comes from studies of individuals experiencing a variety of traumatic circumstances, including natural disasters, plane crashes, health problems and illness, and the loss of loved ones.

Personal Changes: Strength and New Directions

When faced with a significant life challenge, we can develop new self-perspectives. We often gain a greater understanding of our personal strength from surviving a tragedy. We overcome situations that we never thought we could endure. This leads to feeling more self-assured and personally stronger, a confidence that may generalize to different situations, including future challenges.[11] Paradoxically, however, this

---

11   L. E. Thomas, R. C. DiGiulio, and N. W. Sheehan, "Identifying loss and psychological crisis in widowhood," *International Journal of Aging and Human Development*, 26 (1991): 279–295.

often comes hand in hand with an increased sense of vulnerability in acknowledging the uncontrollable nature of hardship and the temporality of our existence.[12]

Surviving traumatic events can push people to hold higher aspirations and achieve greater accomplishments. What encourages these new pursuits after surviving a loss or tragedy? There are a number of possibilities:

- We often restructure our lives in response to traumatic circumstances. Sometimes this restructuring gives us a second chance to fulfill our lost dreams. Such changes can also reveal opportunities that were not present in our previous circumstances.
- We learn that life is meant to be lived to the fullest after surviving trauma. When we are on the other side of tragedy, we realize that we confronted our greatest fear and we survived. As a result, we may be more willing to take calculated risks, which further allow for the possibility of new directions.

Risk is everywhere—it is an unavoidable part of living. In the Jewish perspective, we are commanded to protect our physical bodies, but we are also expected to actualize our potential. To accomplish this, we often have to leave our comfort zone and venture into the unknown. Most of us are afraid and often unwilling to do anything unless we are absolutely certain of success—squandering essential opportunities for growth. Yet, when we experience a traumatic event, it often takes us completely by surprise, reminding us that God ultimately is in control of our fate. This casts the burden on our Creator, allowing us to face our fears and more fully experience the beauty and wonder of this world. As Viktor Frankl said when liberated from the concentration camps: "The crowning experience for all, for the homecoming man, is the wonderful feeling that after all he has suffered, there is nothing he need fear anymore, except his God."[13]

---

12   R. G. Tedeschi and L. Calhoun, "Posttraumatic growth: A new perspective on psychotrauma-tology," *Psychiatric Times*, 21(4) (2004): 58–60.

13   V. Frankl, *Man's Search for Meaning* (London: Rider, 2004), p. 115.

Relationships with Others: Intimacy and Compassion

Closer, more meaningful relationships may also follow when people experience traumatic loss.[14] In normal everyday life, many of us have casual and sometimes superficial relationships with others. When we are overwhelmed with an emotional situation, there is a greater need to talk about our pain. This is not always easy. Many times, we feel diminished and question our own inadequacies and failures. Why did this happen to me? Am I not worthy of being loved? Don't I deserve happiness?

Suffering is humbling but also gives us the freedom to admit that we are fallible, ultimately allowing greater intimacy with others. Sharing our suffering with others also helps us to realize that other people have their own personal anguish, and we develop an increased sense of compassion and greater empathy for others who are suffering. People who are survivors of tragedy often use their pain to bring about positive change for others experiencing similar challenges. Survivors, for example, are often the impetus for establishing foundations and charities for others facing the same circumstances.

According to the Jewish perspective, when we show mercy for another person's suffering, we will be shown mercy from God. Our Sages teach us that if we pray for someone in a similar circumstance as ourselves, then our own prayers will be answered. Several years ago, a friend mentioned that she had been having a very difficult time getting pregnant. She and her husband had been trying for more than two years to conceive a child. She already had two girls but was desperate for another child. Later that same week, another friend with two girls related a similar story to me. The women were friends with each other, but they had never spoken to one another of their own struggles. Separately, I spoke to both women regarding whether they might be interested in praying for someone in a similar situation and both readily agreed. Within a month, each woman was pregnant and both delivered beautiful baby boys—within two weeks of each other! This

---

14   S. E. Taylor, R. R. Lichtman, and J. V. Wood, "Attributions, beliefs about control, and adjustment to breast cancer," *Journal of Personality and Social Psychology*, 46(3) (1984): 489–502.

story not only illustrates the potential power of showing compassion for another person's suffering but also highlights the importance of recognizing our interdependence.

Philosophies of Life: Priorities, Wisdom, and Religiosity

We can also experience changes in our philosophies of life when facing tragedy.[15] When faced with mortality, we develop different priorities. We realize what is most important in life. We understand more clearly that we cannot take our material possessions with us when we die. We are reminded that what remains are our good deeds, including the generosity and loving-kindness that we gave to others.

Suffering can also impart more gratitude and enjoyment in the small pleasures of life. Many people, for example, report having an increased appreciation for their existence and the little things in life such as "child's smile."[16]

A greater sense of existential wisdom can also follow from traumatic events. Three fundamental dimensions of wisdom may be seen as positive outcomes of trauma:[17]

- **Recognizing and managing the inherent uncertainties of life.** People with such wisdom acknowledge the constant nature of change and have an openness to new experiences, both of which enable flexibility when changes happen.[18]
- **Balancing emotions and intellect.**[19] People who can balance their emotions and thoughts are better able to integrate and process their suffering and move forward with their lives.

15   R. G. Tedeschi and L. G. Calhoun, "Posttraumatic growth: Conceptual foundations and empirical evidence," *Psychological Inquiry*, 15(1) (2004): 1–18.

16   Ibid.

17   P. A. Linley, "Positive adaptation to trauma: Wisdom as both process and outcome," *Journal of Traumatic Stress*, 16(6) (2003): 601–610.

18   H. Tennen and G. Affleck, "Personality and Transformation in the Face of Adversity," *Posttraumatic Growth: Positive Changes in the Aftermath of Crisis* (1998): 65–91.

19   D. A. Kramer, "13 conceptualizing wisdom: the primacy of affect-cognition relations," *Wisdom: Its nature, origins, and development* (1990).

- **Accepting the finiteness of life.** This existential acceptance enables us to appreciate the worth, value, and finitude of life,[20] which generates an increased investment in the well-being of others[21] rather than focusing exclusively on ourselves.[22]

For many, an increased religious and spiritual conviction is the most significant positive change when faced with trauma and suffering. Religiosity can be strengthened through reconstructing the meaning of traumatic events in our life and having greater clarity of fundamental existential questions.[23] Although clear answers to existential questions raised by trauma may not be found, the process of wrestling with these issues often produces a deep sense of satisfaction that comes from experiencing life at a more profound level of awareness.[24]

According to the Jewish perspective, God may be more likely to answer our prayers when we develop a deeper level of religious commitment through our suffering. My sister and brother-in-law are an excellent case in point. They had been trying to have a baby for many years, after a series of heartbreaking miscarriages. The community in which they lived continued to grow and eventually needed its own synagogue. My sister and brother-in-law were asked if they would allow their home to be used as the synagogue's residence until proper accommodations could be built. They happily agreed, relishing the opportunity to perform an important mitzvah for the community. They knew what to expect: daily prayer sessions and services on Shabbos, which meant the lack of a living room and some extra cleaning and upkeep. What they did not expect was the change it would inspire in them both. My brother-in-law was now praying with a minyan (quorum of ten men) three times a day.

---

20   P. A. Linley, "Positive adaptation to trauma: Wisdom as both process and outcome," *Journal of Traumatic Stress*, 16(6) (2003): 601–610.

21   E. H. Erikson, (1968) *Identity: Youth and Crisis* (No. 7) (WW Norton & Company, 1968).

22   L. Orwoll and M. Perlmutter, "The study of wise persons: Integrating a personality perspective," *Wisdom: Its Nature, Origins, and Development* (1990): 160–177.

23   K. I. Pargament, D. S. Ensing, K. Falgout, H. Olsen, B. Reilly, K. Van Haitsma, and R. Warren, "God help me:(I): Religious coping efforts as predictors of the outcomes to significant negative life events," *American Journal of Community Psychology*, 18(6) (1990): 793–824.

24   R. G. Tedeschi and L. G. Calhoun, "Posttraumatic growth: Conceptual foundations and empirical evidence," *Psychological Inquiry*, 15(1) (2004) 1–18.

My sister, who was awed by the continual presence of the Torah scroll in her home, successfully avoided performing any activity that might desecrate its presence—such as watching a movie or talking about anyone in a manner that might lead to gossiping. One year later, on the anniversary of the very Shabbos in which the synagogue in their home began, my sister gave birth to healthy twin girls!

POST-TRAUMATIC GROWTH EXERCISE

The Post-Traumatic Growth Inventory was developed by researchers Tedeschi and Calhoun as a way of assessing the positive changes that a trauma survivor may have experienced since the traumatic event.[25] It includes twenty-one statements organized according to the three potential areas of growth and change.

When answering these questions, consider positive changes that you may have experienced in the aftermath of a crisis. For each question, rate on a scale from 0 (not at all) to 5 (a very great degree) the degree to which these changes occurred as a result of this crisis.

	Not at all	A small degree	A moderate degree	A great degree	A very great degree
Relationships					
I have a greater sense of closeness with others.					
I am more willing to express my emotions.					
I have more compassion for others.					
Personal Changes					
I have a greater feeling of self-reliance.					

25   R. G. Tedeschi and L. G. Calhoun, "The Posttraumatic Growth Inventory: Measuring the positive legacy of trauma," *Journal of traumatic stress*, 9(3) (1996): 455–471.

I am better able to accept the way things work out.					
I discovered that I'm stronger than I thought I was.					
I developed new interests.					
I established a new path for my life.					
I am more likely to try to change things that need changing.					
Philosophies of life					
I changed my priorities about what is important in life.					
I have a greater appreciation for the value of my own life.					
I can better appreciate each day.					
I have a better understanding of spiritual matters.					

Here are some additional questions for reflection:

- What strengths did you discover from this experience?
- What new roads or pathways were found?
- How have your perspectives and philosophies changed on what matters in life?
- What strengths (either personal, friends, or family) helped you experience positive growth from this experience?
- What would you tell your past self that would have been helpful during this crisis?

- What would you tell your future self that would be helpful when experiencing a new challenge?

ARE POSITIVE CHANGES IN THE MIDST OF ADVERSITY AN ILLUSION?

When one reports growth and transformation from suffering, are these real changes? Do individuals report changes because they have been led to believe that good must come out of a traumatic event? Is viewing ourselves as stronger in the face of trauma a way of coping, or does it represent an objective change in our personal strength? Are closer relationships indicative of the fact that we rely more on friends and family during times of difficulty, or are we experiencing an authentic transformation in our relationships with family and friends?

Studies show that people who find meaning in their suffering experience better physical and mental health and a lower rate of mortality.

While it may be difficult to untangle the different processes involved in positive growth from suffering, there is too much evidence to dismiss such transformations as mere illusions. What is most convincing is that research has linked positive growth to a better recovery after trauma. A number of studies have found that people who report positive benefits from traumatic circumstances have better mental health; for example, stroke victims had a lower likelihood of experiencing depression,[26] and breast cancer survivors experienced more positive adjustment.[27]

Interestingly, studies have also found that those people who find meaning in their suffering have better *physical* health. A study of men who experienced a heart attack, for example, found that those who perceived benefits from their initial heart attack had significantly better cardiac health and were less likely to suffer a subsequent attack eight years later, even taking into account their age, income, and the severity of their

26   S. C. Thompson, "The search for meaning following a stroke," *Basic and Applied Social Psychology*, 12(1) (1991): 81–96.
27   S. E. Taylor, R. R. Lichtman, and J. V. Wood, "Attributions, beliefs about control, and adjustment to breast cancer," *Journal of Personality and Social Psychology*, 46(3) (1984): 489.

initial attack. In another study, bereaved HIV-positive men who found meaning in their suffering maintained higher levels of their CD4 (helper) T cells compared to other men who failed to find meaning in their loss.[28] The discovery of meaning in suffering was also related to a lower rate of mortality for these men. Only three out of the sixteen men who found meaning died in the follow-up period, whereas half of those who did not find meaning died.[29] Overall, these findings suggest that finding meaning in suffering not only has psychological benefits but may also contribute to better physical health and longevity for those experiencing trauma.

There are several reasons why finding meaning in traumatic circumstances may reinforce better psychological and physical recovery:

- Positive emotions have been shown to affect our physical state. For example, a study of stressed law school students found an association between optimism and a higher number of CD4 (helper) T cells.[30]

- Positive emotions may similarly promote more conscious behaviors. People who have more self-confidence and greater optimism, for example, practice habits that enhance physiological and psychological health such as exercise, and avoid negative habits such as smoking.[31]

- High-quality social relationships likewise have been linked to better psychological and physiological health. When people have friends and family to rely on, they tend to feel better about themselves and are less stressed in the face of difficult circumstances.

- People with more psychological and social resources may also be more apt to guard against or offset stressful events before their full implications take hold.

---

28 S. E. Taylor, M. E. Kemeny, G. M. Reed, J. E. Bower, and T. L. Gruenewald, "Psychological resources, positive illusions, and health," *American Psychologist*, 55(1) (2000): 99–109.

29 Ibid.

30 S. C. Segerstrom, S. E. Taylor, M. E. Kemeny, and J. L Fahey, "Optimism is associated with mood, coping, and immune change in response to stress," *Journal of Personality and Social Psychology*, 74(6) (1998): 1646.

31 S. E. Taylor, M. E. Kemeny, G. M. Reed, J. E. Bower, and T. L. Gruenewald, "Psychological resources, positive illusions, and health," *American Psychologist*, 55(1) (2000): 99–109.

Within Judaism, we are taught to take a proactive approach to our suffering. Our Sages teach us to initiate specific changes when experiencing tough times in order to speed up their positive resolution. We have the possibility to change our fate through three essential actions: *teshuvah*, *tefillah*, and *tzedakah*. Does this mean that through these three actions we change God's mind about our fate? Not quite. When we engage in *teshuvah*, *tefillah*, and *tzedakah*, we transform ourselves. These three actions evoke a process of healing that rectifies the imbalance between our physical and spiritual elements. They ensure that the physical does not dominate our lives and cause suffering, but rather is used as a tool to elevate the spiritual. When we accomplish this through *teshuvah*, *tefillah*, and *tzedakah*, we essentially render our suffering unnecessary. In this sense, the very process that heals our suffering can also serve to eliminate the need for it.

The essential meanings of *teshuvah*, *tefillah*, and *tzedakah* are often misunderstood. *Teshuvah* is sometimes deemed to be repentance. *Teshuvah*, however, means returning or going back to the place where we have been before. The underlying concept of *teshuvah* is that we are essentially good, but our worldly desires obscure our true nature. *Teshuvah* is the process of returning to our destined path, in accordance with God's plan. This path leads to the completion of our unique purpose, which we fulfill through our own improvement and self-refinement. God does not expect us to be perfect. We will certainly have lapses of judgment and slip-ups as we move along our way. *Teshuvah* allows us to be forgiven by God, while learning and growing from our mishaps and missteps.

According to the *Shaarei Teshuvah* ("Gates of Repentance"), there are several stages of *teshuvah*, some of which include regretting what we have done wrong, resolving never to repeat the action, confessing the action with true regret, correcting the action as much as possible, and not repeating the action when the opportunity arises. [32] *Teshuvah* therefore can eradicate one of the primary purposes for suffering in the

---

32   Rabbeinu Yonah of Gerona.

first place, which is to spiritually cleanse ourselves—rediscovering our innermost goodness.

Tefillah is often translated as prayer, yet *tefillah* means to attach oneself. If we pray only to ask God for what we lack, we may consider prayer redundant if we don't particularly need or desire anything at a given moment. *Tefillah*, however, has the primary purpose of increasing our attachment to God and establishing a continuous relationship with our Creator. *Tefillah* nourishes our souls, allowing our spirituality to preside over our physical desires. *Tefillah* therefore serves as a daily reminder of our ultimate purpose in this world.

Tzedakah is often considered charity; however, this translation is inappropriate since the word implies a voluntary act of financial or practical assistance. Rather, *tzedakah* means righteousness or justice. The implication is that *tzedakah* is an obligation. When we are dominated by our physical side, we put our own needs and desires first. *Tzedakah* puts the needs of others at the forefront, redirecting our physical desires, which are naturally inclined toward self-absorption and egoism. *Tzedakah* also confirms our partnership with God. When we give to others, we are emulating God. In accordance with "measure for measure," God bestows freely to us in return. Therefore, *tzedakah* serves both as a remedy and prevention for our suffering.

ARE LIFE CHALLENGES NECESSARY FOR GROWTH?

While resilience can only occur in the face of life challenges, suffering is not the only path toward self-actualization. Research finds, for example, that people who do not experience any exceptionally stressful events also report self-improvement, although at a lower level than those who are trauma survivors.[33] Rather than resulting from a catalyst event, positive growth may happen gradually with an accumulation of life experiences. This

> Suffering is not the only path toward self-actualization; we can also grow from joyous events and life experiences.

---

33   R. G. Tedeschi and L. Calhoun, "Posttraumatic growth: A new perspective on psychotrauma-tology," *Psychiatric Times*, 21(4) (2004): 58–60.

may be particularly true for individuals who are reflective and geared toward personal growth.

Joyous events can likewise lead to positive life changes. Researchers, for example, have noted that there is an increase in religiousness following marriage and child rearing.[34] These events often involve a restructuring of our life and challenge our previous assumptions about ourselves and our relationships with others. These changes, accompanied by the emotional aspects of loving and creating, can produce personal growth and transformation, motivating us to become better individuals for the sake of our spouse and children.

Peak experiences can also be catalysts for self-realization.[35] Peak experiences are defined as especially joyous and exciting moments in life, involving sudden feelings of intense happiness and well-being, wonder and awe, and possibly awareness of transcendental unity and knowledge of higher truth.[36] Peak experiences may be inspired by deep meditation, powerful feelings of love, exposure to great art or music, intellectual understanding, or the overwhelming beauty of nature. The psychologist Abraham Maslow describes how peak experiences affirm the meaning and value of existence and provide a sense of purpose to the individual.[37] Peak experiences give a feeling of wholeness and completion. They can be life-transforming and self-improving. However, sustained peak experiences are often the product of hard work, suggesting that these experiences represent a culmination of one's effort, an apex where greater understanding has finally been achieved.

In the Jewish perspective, peak experiences may be akin to moments when truth is revealed. Our Sages teach us that Divine sparks of all the Jewish souls in existence were present at Sinai, witnessing the

---

34   B. Ingersoll-Dayton, N. Krause, and D. Morgan, "Religious trajectories and transitions over the life course," *The International Journal of Aging and Human Development*, 55(1) (2002): 51–70.

35   M. Csikszentmihalyi, "The Domain of Creativity," in M. A. Runco and R. S. Albert, eds., *Theories of Creativity* (Newbury Park, CA: Sage, 1990), pp. 190–212.

36   A. Maslow, *Religion, values and peak experiences* (New York: Viking, 1970).

37   Ibid.

revelation of the Torah.[38] As previously noted, an angel taught us the entire Torah when we were in the womb. In our lives, we are thus simply relearning what we already know. When this happens, we experience "aha moments," when everything fits together. These moments require effort and learning, yet they exist within us, waiting for their revelation.

It is also important to remember that suffering, tragedy, loss, and trauma are not desirable in and of themselves. Judaism does not promote suffering but rather joy. Rabbi Simcha Zissel Ziv of Kelm wrote:[39]

> *Some people mistakenly think that to follow the path of the Torah one must reject everything worldly. They are under the misconception that one must live a life of suffering and deprivation and be submissive to others. However, this is not the Torah's path which is referred to as "a tree of life to all who grasp her and whoever holds onto her."[40] The verse tells us: "Her ways are ways of pleasantness."[41] As it is said: "Contentment is a feast without end."[42]*

---

38 *Devarim* 5:1–4.
39 *Chochmah U'Mussar*, vol. 2, p. 190, cited in *Gateway to Happiness*, p. 24.
40 *Mishlei* 3:18.
41 Ibid., 3:17.
42 Ibid., 15:15.

PERSONAL RESILIENCE PLAN

This final exercise will help you to move forward and consider what changes you wish to implement to build resilience. Review the different strengths that promote resilience that were discussed in this book. For each particular strength, decide whether you are still working on it or whether you have achieved it and are working to maintain it.

	Not there yet... still working on it!	Got it...working to maintain it!
Self-Efficacy: I believe I am capable of handling challenges.		
Learned Optimism: I believe that good things will happen to me.		
Growth Mindset: I believe that learning new things will increase my intelligence.		
Self-Compassion: I give myself the love, care, and forgiveness I need, especially when I am going through a tough time.		
Problem-Solving: I can define a problem, determine its cause, and identify and implement a solution.		

Planning: I can make a plan of action and strategize how best to proceed.		
Positive Reframing: I can reframe challenges to see their positive side.		
Positive Emotions: I experience positive emotions such as awe, amusement, gratitude, love, joy, contentment, compassion, and interest every day.		
Mindfulness: I can focus on what is happening in the moment.		
Hope: I feel hopeful about the future.		
Faith: I have faith in God even when I am tested.		
Meaning-Making: I believe that my challenges have a purpose and meaning.		
Family Relationships: My family is loving and secure.		
Family Communication: My family can talk openly about the problems we are facing without judgment or criticism.		
Family Organization: My family has a flexible but fairly consistent routine and structure.		
Family Worldview: My family shares positive assumptions of the world and our place in it.		
Family Shared Identity: My family has a cohesive shared identity.		

Family Situational Meaning: My family is able to make meaning out of our challenges.		
Friends: I have at least one best friend whom I can rely on in times of difficulty.		
Community: In my community, we support one another.		
Nature: I am able to appreciate and experience the beauty of nature on a regular basis.		

Now, choose one strength that you are still working on.

- What are three actions you can engage in to strengthen this area?
- What prevents your progress in this area?
- What can you do to counter this barrier?
- What supports your progress in this area?
- How can you encourage this support?

Choose one strength you have achieved, which you are working to maintain.

- How can you apply this area of strength more regularly in your daily life?
- What prevents you from applying this strength?
- What can you do to counter this barrier?
- What supports this strength for you?
- How can you encourage this support?

AFTERWORD

Consider this not an afterword but a foreword to the rest of your life. This book was written with the purpose of enablement and empowerment, so you can live your best life possible!

Living your best life does not mean experiencing only comfort and safety. You must live your life as it was meant to be lived, which inevitably includes experiencing pain and joy, failure and success, heartbreak and love, and regression and progression. These opposing forces come hand in hand, but hopefully you will experience more of the latter than the former.

We cannot choose what life has in store for us. But we are taught that God does not give us anything that we cannot handle. Each of us has our own unique journey to follow and we must accept what we are given. At the same time, we decide, either actively or with indecision, how to live this gift of life. You have a tremendous capacity deep within you. You have the entire world of the Torah in your soul.

Consider your life as you would your own precious child. Nurture and love yourself unconditionally, but give yourself wholesome boundaries and consistent structure so that you can truly flourish. Take measured risks to experience life, but, at the same time, be careful to surround yourself with trustworthy, kind, and inspiring people in healthy environments. Strive to reach your potential and share your unique gifts with those who will learn and grow from them. Remember the miracle that is you and appreciate God in everyday moments.

May you go from strength to strength.

ABOUT THE AUTHOR

Dr. Leslie Morrison Gutman is an associate professor in Clinical, Health, and Educational Psychology and the program director of the MSc Behavior Change at University College London. She is also an associate editor of the *Journal of Adolescence* and associate at the Early Intervention Foundation. She received her PhD in Education and Psychology from the University of Michigan-Ann Arbor. Leslie has authored over sixty-five academic publications, including peer-reviewed scientific journal articles, chapters in textbooks, and policy reports for government. She also writes articles for Aish.com. Her research focuses on developmental trajectories in childhood and adolescence, health and well-being, risk and resilience, and aspirations and attainment, as well as the development, implementation, and evaluation of interventions for children, adolescents, and families. She lives in London with her husband and children.

MOSAICA PRESS

BOOK PUBLISHERS

Elegant, Meaningful & Bold

info@MosaicaPress.com
www.MosaicaPress.com

The Mosaica Press team of
acclaimed editors and designers
is attracting some of the most
compelling thinkers and teachers
in the Jewish community today.
Our books are available around
the world.

HARAV YAACOV HABER
RABBI DORON KORNBLUTH